Suffolk Windmills

Brian Flint

The Boydell Press

First published 1979 by The Boydell Press Ltd,
PO Box 9, Woodbridge, Suffolk IP12 3DF

British Library Cataloguing in Publication Data

Flint, Brian
    Suffolk windmills.
    1. Windmills – England – Suffolk
    I. Title
    621.4'5   TH825

    ISBN 0-85115-112-4

Printed in Great Britain by
BAS Printers Limited, Over Wallop, Hampshire

Suffolk Windmills

Drinkstone postmill

Contents

Acknowledgements

In researching for this book both Stanley Freese and I required the assistance of many people and this, almost without exception, was unstintingly given. Individuals too numerous to mention include mill owners and village residents whose recollection of 'the old mill' has often helped to fit one or two pieces into a vast jig-saw puzzle which will never quite be completed.

Particular thanks are due to Messrs Claude Aldridge, Wilfred Clover, George Cook, Arthur Dolman, Peter Dolman, Frank Farrow, R. Hawksley, Chris Hullcoop, G. W. Martin, Peter Northeast, R. G. Pratt, Phillip Unwin, Rex Wailes, Jesse Wightman and the late Harry Wilton.

I would also like to express my appreciation for the help received from the staff of the following public bodies: The libraries of Ipswich, Gt Yarmouth, Halesworth and Lowestoft, the Suffolk Records Office, the old West Suffolk Records Office at Bury St Edmunds, the Society for the Protection of Ancient Buildings, the Ipswich Museums and the Abbott's Hall Museum of East Anglian Life at Stowmarket.

The drawing of Debenham mill is based on an original measured drawing made by A. R. Dew shortly before the mill was reduced to its present height.

The drawing of Pettaugh mill was measured by R. C. Darby in 1956 and drawn by P. Dolman, the missing details at the time of survey being inserted.

The drawing of Minsmere, Eastbridge windpump was measured in 1976–77 and drawn by P. Dolman in 1978.

The dot distribution map is based on the Ordnance Survey and is reproduced by kind permission of that body.

Photographs have been provided by, and are reproduced by kind permission of the following: (page numbers on which photographs appear are given).
Mr C. E. Aldridge, 45 (right upper and left lower); Mr Beer, 45 (left upper); Mr E. E. Burroughes, 29 (lower); Mr W. Clover, 53 (lower); Mr D. Codd, ii; Mr A. Dolman, 29 (upper) and 57 (left); Mrs Fordham, 6 (right); Mr Michael Goodchild, 60; Mr G. Henderson, 37 (right); Mr O. G. Jarman, 17 (left), 22 and 55 (upper) photographed by his father, Mr H. I. Jarman; Mr N. Lock, 23 (right); W. M. Lummis Collection (SRO), 51 (left) photographed by Mr A. Woolford; Norfolk County Library, 37 (left); Mr T. A. Pike, 7 (left); Miss M. A. Pyke, 34 (upper); Mrs N. Rowlands, 33 (right); Mr H. E. S. Simmons, 17 (right); Suffolk County Council and V.M.P. Consultancy, 48; Suffolk Photographic Surveys (SRO), 6 (left), 21 (left), 53 (upper) and 103 (both); Suffolk Record Office, 76; Mrs Turner, 45 (right lower) photographed by Mr A. R. Fisk; Mr P. Unwin, 23 (left); Victoria and Albert Museum, xiv.

Photographs on pages 7 (right), 25, 41, 51 (right), 55 (left lower), 57 (right), 59 (both), 63, 64, 81 (both), 93 (both), 95, 96, 100 (both) and 115 (both) were photographed by Stanley Freese and are now in the author's collection together with those on pages 20 (both), 21 (right), 33 (left), 34 (lower) and 55 (right lower).

Photographs on pages 11 (both), 14 (both), 38 (both), 47, 72 (both), 84 (both), 106 and 119 (both) were photographed by the author.

Finally I would like to pay tribute to my late friend, Stanley Freese, without whose earlier encouragement and my continuing memory of him this book would have never been completed.

Abbreviations

DOE	Department of the Environment
EAM	East Anglian Magazine
ESCC	East Suffolk County Council
NGR	National Grid Reference
OS	Ordnance Survey
SCC	Suffolk County Council (incorporating ESCC and WSCC)
SPAB	Society for the Protection of Ancient Buildings
SPS	Suffolk Preservation Society
SRO	Suffolk Records Office
WSCC	West Suffolk County Council

Preface

A survey of Suffolk windmills was started in the 1930s by the late Herbert Simmons and Stanley Freese. Much material was gathered, but the fact that neither researcher lived in the county, or very near, meant that many enquiries locally had to wait until 1964, when Mr Freese retired to the village of Wenhaston near Halesworth.

Here he was able to pick up the work again and in the summer of 1966 I met him for the first time at Framsden mill where I was helping Chris Hullcoop in the early stages of the restoration.

I had for several years been garnering information on Suffolk windmills and, on the suggestion of Chris, Stanley and I agreed to pool our resources with the intention, eventually, of having our findings published.

As time went on it became apparent that a county as wealthy in windmills as Suffolk had been would provide material for a monumental work far exceeding in size the excellent treatise on windmills of Surrey and Inner London by K. G. Farries and M. T. Mason.

Stanley Freese did not live to see the work completed but died in the knowledge that I would continue with it and seek publication. The present format differs from that originally envisaged in that it makes no attempt to describe every windmill of which we have been able to find evidence nor does it try to illustrate every windmill of which we have located a photograph or drawing.

The intention is rather to describe, in broad terms, the history of windmills in Suffolk and to discuss their technical details both as regards the typical and the peculiar. The photographs are in the main part previously unpublished and are chosen to best illustrate the various features discussed.

For the reader who wishes to research in greater depth a particular aspect of these mills or, perhaps, the windmills in his locality, I have included a gazetteer of all the sites which have come to my notice together with the Ordnance Survey grid reference and the brief details which space will allow.

Brian Flint
Bramford, Ipswich 1977

List of illustrations

Suffolk Windmills

I

Historical Survey

Every student of windmills knows that one of the earliest authentic references to a windmill in England concerns that built by Dean Herbert on his glebe lands at Bury St Edmunds in 1191.[1] Another early reference is to a windmill at Dunwich between 1185 and 1199.[2] Since the earliest mention of a windmill in Europe does not date before c 1180[3] it appears that Suffolk, in the latter half of the 12th century, was to the forefront in technical innovation.

It is thought that between the Domesday Survey (1086) and the outbreak of the Black Death (1348) the population of Suffolk grew from about 70,000[4] to perhaps more than 200,000,[5] during this period being one of the most populous parts of the country.

Of course Suffolk never relied entirely on windpower for grinding wheat into flour. At the time of the Domesday Survey[6] about 250 mills were recorded in Suffolk but these were all water or horse mills and judging from their large number would have been very small structures probably utilising only one pair of stones apiece. In more recent times water power supplemented wind but in an area of low rainfall and slow moving rivers could not hope on its own to satisfy the needs of a growing population.

It is impossible to find out how many windmills were built or standing in the early period but references become increasingly frequent after 1200, a few examples being:

13th century	Bardwell	1283 and c 1300
	Bury St Edmunds 14 Edward I	(1286)
	Clare temp. Henry III	(1216–72)
	Exning 21 Edward I	(1293)
	Framlingham (or near)	1279
	Hartest	1256
	Haverhill	
	Kelsale	1267–8

	Nowton 14 Edward I	(1286)
	Saxtead	1287
14th century	Grundisburgh (2 windmills)	1341
	Hawstead 40 Edward III	(1367)
	Ipswich	1332
	Ixworth	1393–94
	Saxtead	1309
	Stanton	1393–94

What seems certain is that the large population towards the middle of the 14th century would require a considerable number of windmills to supplement the 250 watermills or their successors of the Norman period. These early windmills would have been generally small affairs mostly utilising only one pair of stones each and it seems likely that the number of windmills probably equalled or exceeded that of watermills at this time.

After the Black Death (*c* 1380) the county population probably numbered about 130,000 and a decline in the number of mills at this period was inevitable. Judging by the Hearth Tax Returns the population had grown to only about 142,000 by 1674 whereafter it continued to increase, with only a few setbacks, up until the present time.

That over a period of several hundred years windmills were a common sight is apparent; descriptions such as that of William Cobbett, writing in 1830 of seeing no less than seventeen from one vantage point, could not have been very unusual.[7] As late as about 1900, from the top of Bradfield St George smockmill, one could see *working* Drinkstone, Gedding, Gt Welnetham and Woolpit postmills and Cockfield and Rattlesden towermills. Derelict Rougham postmill was also visible.[8]

It has been stated that windmills followed the earlier watermills and to some extent supplanted them. However, in several instances, the two types co-existed side by side or at least nearby, the windmill generally acting as an auxiliary aid to the watermill. This was so at Brantham, Capel St Mary, East Bergholt (with Flatford Mill), Fornham St Martin, Mill Hill Hadleigh (with Kersey watermill), Polstead and Wickham Market.

In two cases windmills actually stood on top of watermills but this was long ago and no details of their mechanism were recorded. They stood in Thurston and Wenhaston.[9]

Several manuscript maps of the 16th century show windmills in the county but the first printed maps on which they occur are the road maps in strip form which John Ogilby published in *Britannia* in 1675. However these maps show only main routes and make no attempt to show the county as a whole.

John Kirby's map of Suffolk published in 1736, and revised by Joshua and

William Kirby thirty years later, is inaccurate and lacking in detail. However it shows 48 windmills, the majority of which can be identified although this number certainly represents only a fraction of those standing at the time.

Joseph Hodskinson's one-inch to the mile map, surveyed between 1776 and 1783, shows approximately 180 windmills.[10] On their map to the same scale published in 1825, C. & J. Greenwood include 284 symbols indicating a windmill, many of which, (not surprisingly) coincide with windmills shown on Andrew Bryant's excellent map, published the following year at a scale of one-and-a-half inches to the mile. Bryant indicated no fewer than 374 windmills, a figure much more indicative of the number standing at that time than those shown by his predecessors.

The first Ordnance Survey map to include a strip of southern Suffolk appeared in 1805 but was considered insufficiently accurate and was re-surveyed and published, with sheets covering the rest of the county between 1836 and 1838. These maps, to a scale of one-inch to the mile, show no less than 430 windmills[11] serving a population of slightly more than 300,000, but nevertheless neglected to show several that are known to have been standing at that time.

The distribution of windmills favoured the more populous eastern half of the county, their density being about one and one half times that in the west.

Although windmills were still being built in the 1860s and 70s in Suffolk, the number working steadily declined due mainly to the increasing use of steam power and later the introduction of roller-milling together with improved means of transporting flour and grain.

By the time of the first six-inch Ordnance Survey of the area (between 1875 and 1885) the number of windmills shown had dropped to 360 and included quite a few marked 'disused'. These excellent maps however still fail to show a few mills known to have been standing then.

Many windmill owners purchased portable or stationary steam engines, which they could use when becalmed, as indicated by Kelly's Directory for 1900, which lists 211 windmillers of which 122 also used steam. Of course some of these had separate steam powered roller plants or mills with conventional stones and, although the directory does not make the distinction, several of the separate mills as well as auxiliary engines were oil and not steam powered.

Although the number reflects a later decline than in the Home Counties, the new pattern was emerging; and, with the advent of the first World War and milling restrictions, this decline was accelerated. By 1916 the number had halved and ten years later Rex Wailes, on the occasion of his first survey of the county's windmills,[12] found only 59 corn mills still at work. By 1939 the number had diminished to a mere 13,[13] and since the war increasing labour costs contributed to the virtual death of the windmill as a commercial enterprise although a few lingered on to grind animal feedstuffs.

Today well over 100 remains of windmills are still to be found in Suffolk although many of these are but fragments. The windmill might have disappeared altogether eventually if it were not for a resurgence of interest in recent years. The Wind and Watermill Section of the Society for the Protection of Ancient Buildings, the Suffolk County Council and a number of devoted enthusiasts have contributed to ensure that a few representative mills have been preserved and this aspect will be discussed at length in a later chapter.

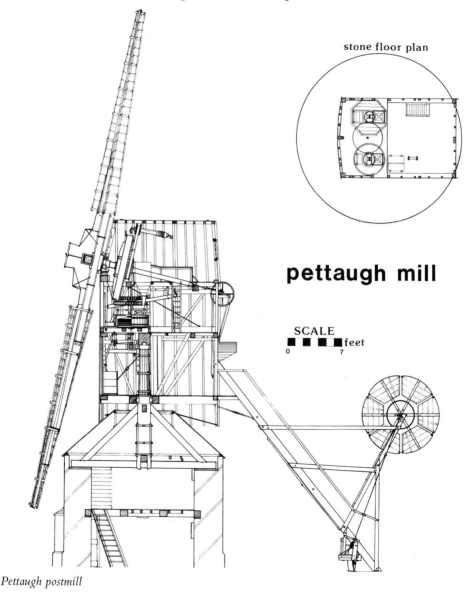

stone floor plan

pettaugh mill

SCALE

0   7 feet

Pettaugh postmill

2

The Postmill

The uninitiated reader will want some explanation of the different types of windmill and may wonder why a machine for pumping water is called a *mill* at all. Strictly speaking a mill is for grinding, but the four-sailed windpump of the marshes bears such a resemblance externally that it has come to be called a windmill like its corn grinding neighbours.

Of the various types we will first consider the postmill, the earliest form and that most frequently depicted in medieval illustrations. The postmill in its infancy was constructed almost entirely of timber, its name deriving from the massive oak post on which the body, or 'buck' as it is called in Suffolk, was supported. The post in turn was supported by the upper ends of four diagonal 'quarter bars' whose feet were mortised into the ends of two horizontal 'cross trees' placed one over the other at right angles.[1] In some early mills the base of this trestle was buried but no evidence of a 'sunken postmill' has come to light in Suffolk. It became standard procedure to elevate the trestle on four brick piers both to avoid rot and gain height and sometimes the structure was built on an artificial mound to better catch the wind. It appears, from an early account, that a ditch was dug around the mound and the earth thrown up onto it, a procedure similar to the construction of a 'motte'.[2] At some time after the destruction of Eye Castle in 1655 a postmill was erected on the castle mound. This lofty siting must have benefited the mill's working but must also have involved a lot of work hauling bags of grain up its steep path. Mill mounds are still to be found at Barking Tye, Barnham, Helmingham, Hintlesham, Hunston, Lakenheath and Lavenham.

The postmill was the most common type in Suffolk doubtless because, in early days, there was plenty of oak available and no local stone which established a tradition which was not broken later when brick towermills were holding sway in Norfolk, Lincolnshire and elsewhere. Of those mills standing in the 1830s whose type we know with certainty almost exactly two thirds were of the post variety, the proportion being slightly higher than this in the east of the county and slightly lower in the west.

Hepworth open-trestle postmill

Badwell Ash open-trestle postmill

The postmill buck was carried on a very heavy horizontal beam called the 'crown tree' which was socketted on top of the post and carried the longitudinal 'side girts' one either side of the buck at first floor level. Sometimes it is found that the side girts do not extend to the tail of the buck and this is taken as evidence that the mill has been extended in length since originally built. Examples of pre-eighteenth century mills are rare but from what evidence remains it appears that the framing of early postmills differed in that there were no side girts, the weight of the structure being transferred to the ends of the crown tree through vertical members extending to the upper and lower side rails. Drinkstone mill alone exhibits this feature amongst those remaining.

It is not known at what date the roundhouse was introduced to give weather protection to the trestle timbers and provide additional storage space. The writer has seen a sixteenth century illustration of a French postmill with roundhouse, so it is quite possible that some mills here exhibited this feature at a time when the 'open trestle pattern' was still the norm. From the eighteenth century onward, postmills were usually built with a roundhouse incorporating the brick piers which were often blended into the roundhouse walls and plastered to give a smooth, easily cleaned surface. Several mills waited until the nineteenth and even early twentieth centuries for roundhouses to be added, some examples being Drinkstone *c* 1830, Framsden 1836, Wenhaston 1851, Eye-Cranley Green 1853,

Westhall 1879, Hitcham after 1881 and Girlings Mill, Swefling and Walpole both
c 1901.

The most common material for roundhouses was brick but flint and brick was
not unusual, that at Syleham being rendered outside. Wooden roundhouses are
known to have existed at Allwood Green Gislingham, Weston and Chippenhall
Green, Fressingfield, the latter being octagonal in shape while the mill near Moats
Tye at Combs had a brick roundhouse with wooden upper storey. Kersey's mill
on Mendlesham Green had a roundhouse of clay lump.

Roofs were usually of tapered boards covered with felt or canvas but several
were tiled, that at Great Mill, Wickhambrook being plastered inside.
Shadingfield and Westleton had particularly attractive roofs of scalloped slates,
while the old postmill on Rougham Common latterly carried a thatched roof.
Occasionally roundhouse roofs were furnished with dormer windows as at Eye,
Gt Barton, Haverhill and Rickinghall Inferior.

One point worth mentioning is that the floor was sometimes excavated below
the level of the surrounding ground to increase headroom. The advent of the tall,
multi-storey roundhouse will be discussed later.

If we wish to go inside the buck of a postmill to inspect the framing and
machinery we must climb the long steps leading up at the rear. An interesting
feature peculiar to Suffolk postmills, and those near the borders of Norfolk and
Essex, will be noted when arriving at the top when it will be seen that the step
strings (side beams) are fitted into slots half way up the door posts thereby
providing a platform which makes entering and leaving the buck a much safer

Gedding postmills

*Postmill on Chippenhall Green, Fressingfield
1934*

7

and more convenient procedure than elsewhere where the step strings are hinged at the rear end of the bottom floor like the tail-board of a cart.

As well as a platform, most Suffolk postmills had an attractive porch cover which, apart from providing some protection from the weather, imparted character to the mill. A study of the illustrations will give some indication of the variety of these porch covers.

On entering the buck it will be noted that the framing includes diagonal members which serve to minimise distortion when the joints eventually weaken. This seemingly obvious refinement was common in Southern England, but not so in the Midlands where mills consequently were often less long lived.

> *I'm round yet I'm flat*
> *I travel with speed,*
> *I go on a good pace*
> *the hungry to feed,*
> *I've been in use for a number of years,*
> *I have a good eye, but I never shed tears,*
> *My back it is broad*
> *my face is the same,*
> *and I guess there's not many*
> *can tell you my name!*
> . . . . A millstone.[3]

The millstones were nearly always situated on the second floor of the buck. In medieval postmills, which were generally quite small, only one pair of millstones was provided, situated forward of the post in the breast or head of the mill. The upper or 'runner' stone was driven by a gear pinion which meshed with the large head-wheel carried on the oak 'windshaft' which also carried the sails at its forward end. Later a second pair of stones in the tail end of the mill was driven by a second pinion or 'stone nut' in mesh with a 'tail wheel' on the windshaft. Another innovation was the provision of a contracting wooden brake which operated on the rim of the head wheel which then became known as the 'brake wheel'.

The introduction of cast iron into millwork from the mid-eighteenth century and increasingly so after the Napoleonic wars enabled several improvements to be made. It became common practice to mount two pairs of stones in the head thereby leaving room at the rear end for ancillary machines such as a dresser for sifting and grading the flour. To do this a spur gear drive was inserted between the 'wallower' (as the first driven gear in a mill is called) and the stones which were placed side by side in the head of the mill. In the nineteenth century most postmills were built thus whilst other earlier examples with head and tail stones were refurbished using iron shafts and gears. It so happened that the buck was sometimes hardly wide enough for two pairs of stones side-by-side and an excrescence or 'pannier' had to be constructed on one side to accommodate the new arrangement. This feature was to be seen on both Framsden mills as well as at Peasenhall and for a time on Cole's Mill, Stradbroke. Parham, Peasenhall and the present Framsden mill were equipped with offset upright shafts whilst the brake wheel cogs were 'hypoidal' to suit the off-centre wallower. This would not have been necessary had a pannier been constructed on both sides of the buck. Large, mostly nineteenth century postmills were sometimes equipped with three pairs of stones, two in the head and the third pair driven by a tail wheel. Examples stood at Bedingfield, Brandeston, Earl Soham, Elmsett, Grundisburgh, Henley, Honington, Ipswich (Anglesea Road), Mendlesham (Kent's Mill), Stanton Chair, Stradbroke Barley Green, Swilland, Wangford, Wickhambrook (Fuller's Mill) and Yoxford.

Examples still stand at Friston (stones now removed), Stanton (with tailstones driven by bevels from the dresser drive) and Ramsey just over the Essex boundary near Harwich. This mill was built at Woodbridge in Suffolk and moved to its present site in 1842, and I always think of it as a Suffolk mill.

Butley, Darsham and Ubbeston postmills had two pairs of stones in the head and a third pair beneath on a hurst frame on the first floor. Hoxne mill was said to have had two pairs in the head and one pair at one side belt-driven. The mill in Castleton Way, Eye which collapsed in 1955, and whose remains are still heaped up around its beautifully carved post, was unique in having a single pair of stones in the head but two pairs in the tail. Having said this it should be borne in mind that details of only a fraction of the mills which once stood in the county have been recorded.

One postmill at Framlingham was equally unusual in having all three pairs in the head on one floor whilst the big mill at Blaxhall had no less than four pairs, two in the head and two in the tail. There was some evidence that Swilland mill may have been fitted with a second pair of tail-stones at one time but Mr Jesse Wightman, who worked on many East Suffolk mills, was of the opinion that it had not.

Although Peak, Cullin and composition stones were sometimes used the majority of millstones were of French *Burr*, built up from sections of stone, cemented together and constrained with shrunk-on iron hoops. These were favoured for flour-milling due to their hardness but many finished their working days grinding animal feed after flour production had become the province of engine-driven roller mills in dock areas of ports such as Ipswich.

Sizes of stones varied from 3 ft (914 mm) diameter to 5 ft 3 ins, (1.6 m) but 4 ft (1.22 m) or a little larger were most common. Although many mills were modernised about a third retained the old 'head-and-tail' arrangement and of those with stones side-by-side in the head the two methods of driving; *overdrift* with the spur gears above and *underdrift* with the gearing below the stones, found about equal favour.

The stones were geared to run at about 100 to 140 rpm, at Framsden for example attaining 100 rpm, at a sail speed of about 13 rpm (overall gearing 7.8:1). Head-and-tail mills, with direct gearing, were often slow runners as it was difficult to obtain such a high ratio with only one pair of gears. However, this was more of a disadvantage with the slower running large shuttered sails than with the fast running little old cloth sailers.

An interesting postscript concerns the unearthing quite recently of fragments of millstone buried near eighteenth century gravestones in Benhall churchyard.[4] It is possible that the graves were those of millers.

Millstones ran with a very small gap between the mating faces and as the windspeed fluctuated even patent sails varied their speed to some degree. The supply of grain to the stones, which was controlled partly by the vibration of the feed shoe against the damsel or the quant and partly by a cord attached to the shoe to alter its inclination, also varied and as the speed increased the runner stone tended to lift. In order to grind properly the gap between the stones had to be regulated. In early days this adjustment, called tentering, was done by hand and in many watermills, with their steadier power source, this remained a satisfactory method. In windmills however constant re-adjustment was required and the introduction of lag-type and centrifugal governors for this purpose in the late eighteenth century was another long needed improvement.

The most common arrangement recorded in Suffolk postmills was to have one governor for each pair of stones belt-driven from the stone spindle. Less commonly the drive was from the upright shaft and was the method adopted at Girling's mill, Swefling while at Peasenhall, Framsden and Saxtead[5] one governor controlled both pairs of stones. In Parham and Worlingworth New Mill the governors were mounted on the stone spindles and at Friston and Swilland the head stones had this arrangement but the tail-stone governor was belt-driven from the upright shaft.

Although the main milling process was concerned with the stones just described many windmills contained auxiliary machines. The process of sifting the meal and grading the flour was at one time the province of the baker and was done by hand but eventually mechanical devices were introduced to perform this task. The bolter, consisting of an inclined cylindrical reel covered with a tubular woven bolting cloth and enclosed in a wooden casing, is said to have been designed in 1502. It was gradually improved but the bolting cloth, of wool or silk, always suffered from attack by moth.

Another dressing machine, known as a wire machine, was invented in the eighteenth century. This was similar in appearance to the bolter and both were to be found mounted across, or in the side of, the tail of many Suffolk postmills.

Framsden postmill; the top floor before restoration

Stanton postmill; stonefloor

Eighteenth and nineteenth century sale notices often described dressers as 'flour mills'. Later mills were built to accommodate a wire machine but often earlier examples were extended by 2 or 3 ft (610 or 914 mm) beyond the rear corner posts as at Framsden and Stanton mills. Drinkstone and Holton mills have been extended at head and tail and there is some evidence that the buck of Drinkstone mill may have been turned end-to-end.

In Framsden, Parham, Thurston and Wenhaston mills the dresser drive was by belt from an iron or wooden skew gear meshing with the brakewheel cogs whereas at Syleham a spur gear meshed with the edges of the iron cogs on the tail wheel. The former arrangement suffered from the disadvantage that the skew gear, unless very accurately made, produced a different wear-pattern from the wallower on the brakewheel cogs and hence shortened their life. A more expensive but better solution was to provide a second row of teeth on the brakewheel for the purpose of driving the flour dresser. This method was used in the mills at Eye, Friston, Grundisburgh and Stanton. In Eye and Friston mills the wooden cogs were mortised into the face of the brakewheel inside the wallower drive whilst Stanton mill has an internal gear with cog segments facing inwards. A similar drive was operated from the tailwheel of Gt Welnetham mill. In Wickhambrook Great Mill a bevel gear drive from the top of the upright shaft above the solid wooden wallower drove the dresser through the usual belt drive with wooden pulleys.

Another sifting device to be found in postmills was the 'jumper' or 'jog-scry'. This comprised a set of reciprocating screens and is known to have been installed in Darsham, Haughley, Stratford St Andrew, Stanton Chair, Thorndon and Friston mills.[6] In the latter it was operated by a cam gear mounted on the windshaft just in front of the tail-wheel, whereas in Haughley mill the drive was from a primitive cog ring formed by screwing wooden bars to the windshaft just in front of the tail bearing. Friston mill also contained an inclined covered sieve under the spout feeding the hopper of one pair of stones together with a funnel in the hopper; this was known as a 'balance-dish'. Other machines to be found in postmills included oat crushers at Grundisburgh, Leavenheath and at Cole's mill, Stradbroke which had no less than five auxiliary machines including a mash mixer and a maize cutter, although several of these were housed in the roundhouse and driven by an oil engine.

As well as flour dressers virtually all postmills incorporated a wind-driven hoist for lifting sacks of grain from ground level to the storage bins on the top floor of the buck. This took the form of a wooden drum sited longitudinally in the roof and turned by a leather belt from a large pulley mounted on the front or rear face of the brakewheel. The belt, which was normally slack, was tightened when required by pulling a cord which either raised the drum as can be seen at Framsden and Syleham or, less frequently, pressed a jockey pulley against the belt thereby tensioning it as at Saxtead. Drinkstone and Stanton mills have a chain in place of the usual belt while at Westhall a spur gear meshed with the inside of the brakewheel cogs to drive the sackhoist and a flour dresser in the tail. Another item of equipment sometimes found in a postmill was a capstan used for lifting and turning over the runner-stones for dressing. Framsden mill still exhibits such a device and one was also to be seen in Pettaugh mill.

Finally we must mention the 'bell alarm' whose purpose was to warn the miller that the grain hoppers were running low and required replenishment. Unfortunately in derelict mills the bell is one of the first items to find a new owner but the device is still to be seen in working order in Framsden and Saxtead mills, although in the former it is a replacement.

Going outside the mill again we will look at that most obvious windmill feature—the sails; and *sails* they are in this part of the country, the term 'sweeps' being used only in counties south of the river Thames. Early illustrations show the sails to have been wooden frames with cloth covering which was laced in and out of the transverse bars of the sail-frames. The frames were attached to either end of the two main supporting timbers called the stocks which were mortised at right angles to one another through the end of the wooden windshaft. The sail frames were inclined at an angle to the stocks so as to rotate in the wind but this angle was constant along their length—there was no 'twist' to the sail. Eventually millwrights realised that greater efficiency would ensue by varying the angle of twist or 'weather', decreasing it from the heel to the tip, typical figures being twenty five degrees at the heel and five degrees at the tip for the two remaining (patent) sails on Framsden mill. John Smeaton reached similar conclusions by experiment in the middle of the eighteenth century and this type of sail became known as the 'common sail'. The sail cloths were no longer threaded through the frames but spread over the windward face of the frames and furled according to the strength of the wind. The disadvantage was that the sails had to be furled by hand from the ground so that each sail had to be brought to the bottom in turn and in stormy or frosty weather this could be an unpleasant and indeed dangerous operation. It also meant that the mill was of necessity relatively low so that the sails could be reached from the ground; therefore advantage could not be taken of higher wind speed at greater height. Once the universal pattern, this type of sail, was still to be found on many old postmills early this century. The only examples still to be seen in Suffolk are on Drinkstone mill and Holton mill near Halesworth.

The next improvement came in 1772 when the Scottish millwright, Andrew Meikle, devised the spring sail. This had hinged shutters connected so as to open and close like the shutters of a venetian blind. The movement was controlled by a coil or elliptic spring whose tension could be adjusted. This was varied according to the wind strength and when the wind gusted the shutters would open, thereby 'spilling the wind' and to some extent regulating the speed of the stones. This type

Syleham postmill; tailstones

Syleham postmill; striking chain bollard

of sail still had the disadvantage that it had to be adjusted when stationary and it had less power than a full spread common sail. For this reason the two types were often combined as can be seen at Drinkstone and was the case at Holton mill before the recent restoration when four common sail frames were fitted for lightness. The combination gave good driving power with a degree of self-regulation. On Wattisfield postmill (pulled down in 1914) two common sails were fitted together with two 'patents'. The common sails were further increased in area by the addition of extra frame panels at the ends on the leading sides of the 'whips' or main backbone timbers.

The patent sail was the invention of an East Anglian, William (later Sir William) Cubitt. Born at Dilham, Norfolk in 1785 he was appointed engineer to Ransome and Son in Ipswich in 1812 and with them was responsible, in 1818, for building the old Stoke Bridge which stood until 1924. He installed a treadmill in the prison in Ipswich for the inmates to grind corn and, when the Ipswich Gas Company was formed in 1817, became its first engineer.

His patent for an improved windmill sail dates from 1807 and combined the hinged shutters of the spring sail with a form of automatic control which had appeared previously in a design known as the roller reefing sail. This type is not known to have been used in Suffolk so will not be discussed. The patent sail shutters are coupled by bell-cranks or 'triangles' to a striking rod which passes through the centre of the hollow windshaft to project at the rear. At the rear end a rack and pinion drive shaft bears a wheel which carries an endless chain on which is hung a weight. The weight is varied according to wind strength and, as the striking rod revolves in relation to the rack, this regulation can be effected with the sails turning. At last the way was open to building tall mills with sails swinging many feet above the ground. It should be noted that the chain-wheel was sometimes inside the buck and sometimes outside with the weight hanging at a level accessible from the rear platform. Occasionally, when a mill was extended at the rear to provide room for a flour dresser, the chainwheel was left half-in and half-out of the mill as can still be seen at Framsden. Sometimes as at Aldringham, Syleham, Stradbroke (Skinners), Walberswick, Westhall and Westleton, the chain-wheel was connected to the striking rod by a bollard or drum around which chains were wound. The late Mr H. Sore, miller of Haughley, stated that he believed the patent sails on Wetherden mill were controlled by a large centrifugal governor.

Spring sails were often *single-sided*, i.e. the shutters were arranged on one side of the whip only, whereas the patent sails used on Suffolk mills were typically *double-sided*. They varied in span from about 50 ft (15.24 m) (7 bays of 3 shutters per sail) to perhaps 75 ft (22.86 m) on the big postmills at Laxfield and Saxmundham each of which had 2 sails carrying 32 shutters on either side of the whip. Framsden may again be considered typical having sails of 8 bays, 3 shutters per bay, spanning

64 ft (19.5 m) by 7 ft 6 ins (2.29 m) wide carried on a stock 44 ft (13.4 m) long and 12 ins (305 mm) square at the centre.

The annular sail or wind-wheel was not fitted to any postmill in Suffolk and will be discussed in Chapter 3.

However, another invention concerning windmill sails was the idea of a Sudbury man, Robert Catchpole. This was an air-brake consisting of longitudinal shutters arranged at the outer ends of the sails on the leading edges. They were controlled by the sail shutter mechanism and when the shutters were opened to stop the sails, would act as a spoiler or air-brake. Catchpole's 'skyscrapers', as they were popularly called, fitted to postmills at Combs, Gedding and Wetherden (two mills). Girling's mill at Swefling had what, at a glance, looked like skyscrapers but were actually only fixed boards at the ends of the leading edges of two sails to increase power. It is uncertain whether the frames on the two single-shuttered sails of Sibton mill were for this purpose or were remnants of air-brakes. An attempt to fit air-brakes to Drinkstone mill was made in the 1920s but the project was abandoned.[7]

Another variation concerns the multi-sail mill. Although the use of more than the usual four sails found favour in some counties, notably Lincolnshire, the idea never caught on in Suffolk and not a single example of a multi-sailed postmill has been recorded in the later period here. However, a reference dating back to 1279 has recently come to light regarding a six-sailed mill at or near Framlingham.[2] It is described as something of a landmark and at that date is almost certain to have been a postmill.

A four-sailed mill could not work with three sails as it would be hopelessly out of balance but several mills, having lost a pair of sails due to storm damage, rot or neglect, carried on for a number of years with the remaining two. Examples were the postmills at Brockley Green, Friston, Mendlesham (Ling's mill), Shadingfield, Stanton, Swefling (Girling's), Syleham, Wickhambrook Great Mill and Woolpit. It has been estimated that a two-sailed mill would develop about sixty percent of its power with four sails so a single pair of stones could be easily driven but due to the pulsing effect when the lower sail was in front of the mill body the mill would run less smoothly. In fact the greater the number of sails the smoother the action although if too many sails were fitted, close together, efficiency would suffer due to interference effects between adjacent sails.

The sails of early postmills usually ran clockwise when viewed from the front. This meant that with only the brake wheel and stone nut drive the runner stone ran clockwise, and the dressing of the surface of the stones could more readily be accomplished by a right handed stone-dresser or miller. When spur gear drive was introduced, the extra pair of gears meant that the direction of rotation of the stones was reversed. In order to keep the stone dressing unchanged, it became standard practice for mill sails to run anti-clockwise when viewed from the front;

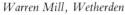

Warren Mill, Wetherden

Framsden postmill in 1934

and those survivors which ran the other way became known as 'left hand mills'. Of course there were exceptions to the rule, Syleham mill being an example of a head-and-tail mill with right hand anti-clockwise sails. Horham mill, the last open-trestle postmill to stand in the county (until 1934), had the tail stone nut driven from the front face of the tail wheel, so that the runner stone ran clockwise. When inside a postmill the sail rotation can easily be checked by reference to the position of the brake lever. In a right hand mill the brake lever will be situated on the right hand side, looking forward, whereas a left hand mill will have its brake lever on the other side.

The other notable external feature of most postmills is the fantail, known as the *fly* or *flyer* in Suffolk. Originally postmills were turned to face the wind by means of a tailpole projecting from the rear. Sometimes, as in the case of Alpheton, Monastic Mill at Leiston, Preston, Redgrave and Fletcher's Mill at Wrentham, a cart wheel was fitted to the end of the tailpole. The tailpole was pushed round by the miller—a very onerous task—or he might hitch his horse to it. Before doing this the miller had to raise the lower end of the steps clear of the ground by means of a lever or 'talthur'. A great improvement was effected when Edmund Lee patented the fantail in 1745. As far as it is known fantails in Suffolk always had six or eight blades, six being more common, and were usually mounted on a frame above the steps with the wheel carriage attached to the bottom of the steps. The 'tramwheels' were nearly always of iron although they were wooden at Elmer's Mill, Woolpit. Various methods of gearing were used between the fantail and tramwheels, the most typical probably being that adopted by the mill-wrighting firm of John Whitmore and Son (later Whitmore and Binyon). Here a single shaft with bevel pinions each end took the drive from the fan spindle down to the wheel carriage, where it meshed with a bevel wheel on a longitudinal shaft within the carriage. This shaft had a bevel pinion at one end which meshed with a gear ring on one of the tramwheels. At the other end of this shaft a pinion meshed with a mate on a similar shaft which was geared to the second tramwheel. It was desirable to drive both wheels to prevent slip and another means of doing this was to drive down to a pair of bevels on an intermediate shaft rather like a car differential half way up the fly-frame. Each bevel was then geared to one of the tramwheels and this arrangement could be seen on Stanton mill. Usually when a tailpole-winded mill was fitted with a fantail the tailpole was retained but cut off at the point where it projected through the steps. When it is remembered that the steps serve as a lever when the fantail turns the mill into wind, the retention of the front portion of the tailpole aids rigidity.

On the Horringer Road mill at Bury St Edmunds and at Wickambrook Great Mill the wheel carriage was mounted on the end of the tailpole; but the fan frame was braced forward to the stop strings, unlike the Sussex pattern, where the whole of the fan carriage was attached to the tailpole which was set further back.

At Ashfield Place, Framsden there stood until *c* 1918 a postmill which was moved from Weybread in the 1880s. On this mill the fan drive was taken by bevels down to a worm gear which meshed with a gear wheel on a single central wheel about 3 ft 6 ins (1.07 m) to 4 ft (1.22 m) diameter. Small outrigger wheels, on either side of the steps, steadied the arrangement. Some time before this mill was dismantled the fan and gearing were put on the composite mill at Monk Soham (see Chapter 3).

Another position for the fan was above the roof of the buck as could be seen, until a few years ago, at Ramsey mill in Essex. Suffolk examples known to us were at Halifax (Ipswich), at Stanton Chair, Swefling and Wortham Ling, while Swilland had this arrangement before being fitted with an ordinary fantail. At Ramsey and Swilland the fantail drive was taken down to a worm ring encircling the post below the buck. Stanton Chair mill evidently drove down to a rack around the top of the roundhouse wall and High Mill, Swefling had a driven wheel on the tailpole end and two outrigger wheels on the steps and two tramways. At Wortham Ling the fan drove the carriage wheels via a long shaft incorporating universal joints.

In view of the fact that both Swilland and Swefling mills finished their working days with conventional fantails it is probable that the roof fan did not function as well as the normal arrangements as well as being rather inaccessible for maintenance.

Tramways were usually of compacted earth or gravel or of concrete. Wooden slabs or bricks were sometimes used whereas the large postmill at Blaxhall, burned in 1883, had an iron tramway which was then transferred to Brandeston mill which suffered a similar fate ten years later. It was finally taken to Pettaugh mill.

As with roundhouses, fantails were sometimes fitted quite late in a mill's life. One of the postmills at Hopton was 'made to turn itself into the wind' in 1824[8] while Wangford postmill had to wait until after 1895 to be so modernised, as did Gedding mill which had the fly from Coddenham mill in 1905. Old Drinkstone mill had an even longer wait, being tailpole-winded for the best part of three centuries until in the 1940s its owner, Mr Wilfred Clover, fitted the carriage from Stradbroke, Barley Green Mill with hand cranking gear and in 1963 the fantail using parts from nearby Woolpit mill which had collapsed shortly before.

The advent of iron castings for gears and shafts, together with such improvements as the patent sail and the fantail, both of which depended on small castings for their functioning, led to the development of the fine nineteenth century Suffolk postmills. The building of tall postmills was more typical of East Suffolk than of West (although by no means confined to the former), while they have been described by Mr Rex Wailes as the finest of their type in the world.

Although many mills were built from scratch in the new style, albeit sometimes on the same spot as a more primitive predecessor, others were extensively modernised to extend their useful life at a lower cost than the building of a completely new mill. Of those still standing both Framsden and Saxtead mills were raised on their piers, Framsden having its roundhouse added whilst that at Saxtead was heightened. In both cases iron machinery driving two pairs of stones was furnished by the millwrighting firm of John Whitmore and Son of Wickham Market.

Another tall postmill, of which the grey brick roundhouse remains, stood until 1907 at Saxmundham. This mill is reputed to have been much lower originally and was heightened when surrounding buildings obstructed the wind. A similar problem was experienced by William Goodchild who ran the last windmill at Stoke, Ipswich until 1884. He complained that year by year the mill's power diminished because, as the number of houses in the vicinity increased, so the power of the wind decreased.

Judging from photographs Saxmundham mill must have been at least as high as Friston which measures 51 ft (15.55 m) to the roof ridge and is the tallest postmill still standing in the country. Saxmundham, like Framsden, has the piers blended into the roundhouse wall and does not show evidence of having been heightened.

Another very tall postmill stood, until about 1926, at Drane's Farm, Weybread.

Saxmundham postmill   *Postmill at Drane's Farm, Weybread*

We do not know its precise height but some idea may be gained from the fact that it had no fewer than forty-two steps at the rear whereas Friston mill has but forty. Swilland mill was very large with a broad, tapered roundhouse and thirty-eight steps and stood about 51 ft (15.55 m) high and the postmill which stood on Benhall green until 1921 or 22 had been heightened two or three times and was also a tall mill.

In West Suffolk, Thomas King, the diarist, tells us he walked on the roof tree of Mr Baker's postmill at Stanton on the occasion of its being raised (built) on Saturday, 21st August 1824. He tells us that the height was 48 ft (14.65 m), the same height as the present Framsden mill which has thirty-three steps at the rear— the same number as Pettaugh.

Several large mills, long demolished and not represented by existing photographs, may have vied for the title of 'the tallest postmill in Suffolk'. Blaxhall mill was said to have been very large and tall as was Henley mill built in 1810, heightened in 1837 and finally suffering the fate of many mills, being burnt down on 27th November 1884.[9] The 'Great' or 'Black Mill' was brought from Southtown, Yarmouth in 1798 and erected on the edge of Southwold Common. A photograph taken about 1860 shows it then with fairly low roundhouse, wooden windshaft and two patent sails to supplement two long commons. Although a fantail was fitted the original tailpole was still its full length, projecting through the steps. In 1863 the mill was extensively damaged in a gale

Southwold Black Mill, c 1860   *Southwold Black Mill after rebuilding*

and afterwards modernised as later photographs show it with tall roundhouse, iron windshaft and four patent sails. The tailpole was cut off at the steps and the small windows in the sides of the buck replaced with larger sash windows; a steam engine was housed nearby. In its new guise the 'Great Mill' (so called to distinguish it from its lesser neighbours in the town) had a short life, being dismantled in 1894.

Of those mills documented, Honington and Thorndon postmills claimed pride of place as the highest in Suffolk.[10] They are both reputed to have been 55 ft (16.77 m) high and the tall roundhouses still stand, the former converted into a house and the latter still containing its trestle. Honington mill has been down many years but Thorndon stood until 1924, being demolished after it was struck by lightning the previous autumn.

Although postmills in England may have been built as tall as 55 ft, a careful analysis of the existing photographs of Thorndon mill, together with the extant remains, leads to the conclusion that it had fewer than 40 steps at the rear and that the height of the buck ridge from ground level did not exceed 52 ft (15.85 m). It is safe to say, I think, that 'they didn't come much bigger than Friston'. There was said to have been some competition to own the tallest postmill as the same millwright who raised Thorndon mill to its great height in 1820 was commissioned to do the same for the postmill on the later towermill site at Debenham. However, in this instance the project was unsuccessful as the mill toppled over, injuring one of the workmen, and was smashed.

It is probable that nearly all early postmills were constructed almost entirely of

Great Barton postmill

locally grown oak, well seasoned and capable of resisting the ravages of weather and wood beetle for a great number of years. Even the buck boarding was likely to have been hardwood and oak sailstocks would not have been uncommon. In order to provide long sailstocks for carrying large patent sails, long-grained coniferous timbers were later favoured, pitch pine being shipped from the Americas although a Russian fir, exported through the Baltic port of Memel, now Klaipeda, was considered superior being lighter although equally strong.

Oak of course was in demand for house and barn building and by the shipyards on the River Orwell so by the last century was in comparatively short supply. In most nineteenth century postmills a goodly amount of pitch-pine was used although oak was still nearly always used for the trestle and other main structural timbers such as crown-tree and side-girts.

If Framsden mill is examined it will be found that the original framing, dating from about 1760, is of oak and lightly built as would have befitted a typical mill of that date with common sails and tailpole winding. When modernised in 1836 pitch-pine was introduced for the sprattle-beam (at the upper end of the upright

Hoxne postmill   *Thorndon postmill c. 1900*

shaft), tail–beam (supporting the rear end of the windshaft) and bridge–trees (supporting the stone spindles).

The postmill on Benhall Green was very unusual, being largely of sweet chestnut including the post while St Michael South Elmham mill had an elm crown tree.

We do not know whether medieval mills were painted for protection; the timber may well have been left to weather naturally. Judging by Cobbett's description of mills around Ipswich in 1830,[11] and paintings and engravings of that period, the majority were, by then, painted white and there is no doubt a white postmill is by far the prettiest. However, the cost of having to repaint a postmill every few years with white lead paint was sometimes found prohibitive and tar or creosote was substituted, giving rise to the name 'Black Mill' in several instances. Roundhouses were often tarred or sometimes painted but for appearance a good red brick could not be bettered.

Sailframes were usually painted white and fantail blades were traditionally blue in Suffolk although red, white and blue on alternate vanes of six bladed flys was to be seen on several mills this century—doubtless a patriotic gesture. A few millers, maybe wishing to express individuality, painted their mills in unconventional colours such as Thurston which had red sails and fly. Mr William Greenard at Worlingworth New Mill in the 1930s had it tarred black with a white tail and black and white roundhouse. Sails and steps were the usual white but the fly was yellow. Incidentally, the roundhouse standing there today belonged to this mill's earlier neighbour.

The use of cast iron in millwork has been alluded to with reference to gearing and the production of small castings but two further instances of its use are worth recording. One was the provision of a 'Samson-head' or reinforced capping for the post. This was invariably an addition to extend the life of an ailing post and, at the same time, an iron flange was attached to the underside of the crowntree to provide a bearing. A Samson-head was fitted to the posts of Clowes Corner mill at Earl Soham, Parham, Thornham Magna and Wickhambrook Great Mill and is still in evidence in Drinkstone and Saxtead mills.

Cast iron windshafts became standard in the nineteenth century and were fitted as replacements for wooden ones in many mills but an alternative was to re-use a wooden shaft by cutting off the weak or broken head end, through which the sail-stocks were mortised, and fitting an iron canister. This style of windshaft is installed in Drinkstone and Stanton mills and was also fitted in the postmills at Debenham, Gt Welnetham, Hartest, Haughley, St Michael South Elmham, Thornham Magna and Woolpit.

With a wooden windshaft the brakewheel and tailwheel (if fitted) were in early days made up with radial arms which were passed through mortices in the shaft. This arrangement weakened the shaft and of course, could not easily be applied to an iron shaft unless the shaft was unnecessarily large from a strength point of view. The 'compass arms' as they are called, would also interfere with the passage of the striking rod of patent sails.

However, before the advent of iron windshafts, an alternative design with the wheel arms clasped around the shaft and wedged, became popular and was to be found latterly in nearly all postmills. Quite often a compass-arm wheel was converted to clasp-arm, the original compass arm sockets still being visible in the brake wheel cants of Drinkstone and Framsden mills as they used to be at Barley Green Stradbroke, Gedding and Haughley. Several iron brake wheels were in evidence when Rex Wailes and Stanley Freese made their surveys before the last war, Parham mill having a wooden rimmed wheel with iron boss and eight arms.[12]

As has been indicated windmills often were given names, usually to distinguish one from another in the same village or locality. The most common distinction was to use the miller's name, a mill often staying in the same family for many years. The appellations High Mill, Old or New Mill and Black or White Mill are self-explanatory. Little Kitty Mill at Wickhambrook may have been so called through a feeling of affection as may have Kitty Mill, Wenhaston. Haverhill Castle Mill took its name from the nearby earthworks whereas the name Monastic Mill pointed to the fact that this old postmill at Leiston, demolished *c* 1870, belonged to the abbey there until the dissolution. Gothic Mill, Halesworth,

Wenhaston postmill and miller, Dick Spencer in May 1938

believed to be a postmill, was said to take its name from the nearby Gothic House. Victoria Mill, Eye was so called after the name of the road nearby. At Southwold the White Mill, standing on the common, was also called the Town Mill and Corporation Mill as it belonged to the borough and was leased to millers. The more easterly of the two postmills at Walton was known as Wadgate Mill after the small hamlet in which it stood fulfilling a dual purpose, not only producing flour for the neighbourhood but serving as a leading mark for mariners.[13]

Names were occasionally denoted on eighteenth and nineteenth century maps, the postmill at Rickinghall Inferior being called North Mill on Hodskinson's map. Greenwood named Castle Mill on the mound at Eye and on Bryant's map the postmill near Moats Tye, Combs was called Branstead Mill and the westerly mill at Wetherden was named as Warren Mill. On the same map the mill, known later as Page's at Debenham, was then Gowd's, Gt Barton postmill was named Morris's and the postmill in Foxhall Road, Ipswich was marked as Goodwin's Mill. Bryant also named Cross Mill at Cross Green, Hitcham and Upper Mill, being the southerly of the two at Brundish, and he distinguished two of the three postmills at Stradbroke by the names Barley Mill and Battlesey Mill after the greens on which they stood. The old series Ordnance Survey one-inch map in the town of Beccles distinguished Ingate Mill, a postmill wrecked in a storm in 1879, and named Warren Mill, Wetherden. At Hundon it showed Brockley Mill (latterly Ruses) and at Glemsford was Weston Mill but what type this was is not known. In the area of that name in Ipswich was placed Bolton Mill and in Great Ashfield the curious title Baten Haugh Mill was appended to the usual windmill symbol. An interesting fact concerns the Turning Mill shown on the same map at Snape. An octogenarian questioned before the last war said he had been told it was a windmill used for turning children's toys, and this without being prompted with the name. Recently I have learnt that it was built by a wood turner *c* 1828 on a tumulus.[14]

The Ordnance Survey maps also marked a number of earlier windmill sites such as Mill Hill at Bacton and at Wickham Skeith, Mellfield Wood at Bradfield St George and Millfield Wood at Polstead. Mill Mount was to be found at Chattisham, Helmingham, Redisham and Wetheringsett. That at Redisham is an early earthwork and may well have had a postmill on its summit in the past. Greenwood showed Mill Tye at Gt Cornard as did the 1805 Ordnance Survey map; a *tye* was another name for a common. Greenwood's map also shared with the 1837 OS the distinction of showing Mill Hill Farm at Hitcham. At Westhall the 1837 map showed Millpost Cottage and at Wenhaston marked Mill Heath. Later map references as well as existing names of farms, lanes and cottages attest to the memory of vanished windmills of which we generally know more than of those just mentioned.

But returning to postmill names; perhaps the most endearing was accorded to

High Mill at Swefling. Windmills, like ships, were (and indeed still are) referred to as *she*, although I have refrained from addressing them so in this book as the term becomes tiresome with repetition. However, this mill went one better, being given a girl's name—Rachael.

As well as being given names mills often bore dates and inscriptions. Sometimes the year in which the mill was built was carved on a beam or on the post and intitials of the owner were appended.

The earliest recorded date was either 1615 or 1516 on the crowntree of the little old mill which stood on Allwood Green, Gislingham until *c* 1885. Seventeenth century dates were to be seen in Hudson's mill, Snape (1668), Skinner's mill, Stradbroke (1688) and Pyke's mill, Woolpit (1644) while Drinkstone mill bears the date 1689 with the initials 'S.S.' Not unnaturally many more eighteenth century dates have been recorded, Botesdale Lodge Mill being date 1777, Laxfield 1769, Rougham 1774, Girlings mill Swefling 1775, Thornham Magna 1750 and Wickambrook Great Mill 1740 and 1790. Eye mill post still carries the finely carved date 1779 and inscription 'MSA RW Fecit'. On the left side-girt of Framsden mill appears the legend 'Carter I Cross 1794' although we know the mill to have been standing before 1783 and Mr Cross does not appear as the owner in the deeds. Fressingfield Chippenhall Green mill bore carvings of an open trestle postmill with the dates 1712 and 1847 and of a smockmill with the date 1792 and name R. Bottright. Mill Hill mill at Halesworth was inscribed 'IC 1788' while Hartest mill also carried an indeciperable date of the 1780s. The visitor to Holton mill will find a profusion of names and dates, the earliest apparently 'F + Swan 1749'. In Cole's mill at Stradbroke was proclaimed 'I + F 1777', the piece of wood carrying this inscription still being in the possession of Mr Cole. The easterly of the two postmills on Stoke Hill, Ipswich, which has been mentioned previously, carried an iron weathervane pierced with the date 1786. This now resides in the Christchurch Mansion museum.

Coming up to the nineteenth century we find the date 1855 (or possible 1835) in Friston mill although the mill or a predecessor was standing here in 1812.[15] Haughley mill, built in 1811, bore the inscription 'J. T. Bird 1840' and St Michael South Elmham mill, built in 1799, was dated 1827. One of the mills at Hopton is said to have been dated 1806 and Darsham,[12] Parham, Peasenhall and Westleton mills were dated 1801, 1821, 1803 and 1851 respectively. Parham and Peasenhall mills may well have been built at these dates but Westleton postmill was standing in 1842 being shown on the tithe map of that date although not appearing on the Ordnance Survey of five years previously. On the post of Stanton mill is carved 'RRIX 1807'.

The roundhouse at Framsden has scored in the brickwork in two places the date 1836 as had that at Westhall (1879) whereas at Wenhaston Kitty Mill a wall tie-plate gave the date of building the roundhouse as 1851. Iron windshafts were occasionally dated, that at Pettaugh being 1865 whilst the one in Saxtead mill has cast on it. 'JOHN WHITMORE WICKHAM MARKET SUFFOLK 1854'.

It only remains to describe a few peculiarities which distinguished certain postmills from their more prosaic neighbours. Perhaps the most remarkable in external appearance was that at Gt Welnetham, often called Stanningfield mill. This was derelict in the 1920s but was then repaired and put back to work by Mr Marriage of Bury St Edmunds who fitted a bowsprit projecting from the canister and tied back to the tips of the sails with strainer wires.

This mill also boasted a gallery around the top of the buck, a feature also to be seen on Bradwell mill while at Holton a platform across the rear of the buck at upper floor level, together with an access door, was added when the machinery was removed and the mill used as a summer house shortly after the turn of the century.

Warren Mill, Wetherden, as well as being fitted with Catchpole's 'skyscrapers' was notable in two other respects. Although not a particularly tall mill it had two braces from the rear corner posts of the buck to the bottoms of the step strings. In addition to a flat porch cover it had an upper porch to protect the striking gear for the sails. Coddenham mill, which was rather taller, had similar step braces, but extending to a point only about half-way down the strings and was also equipped with a striking gear cover but extending the full width of the buck. At Framsden the striking gear chain-wheel, which partially projects is covered by a box or 'beehive' while the end of the rack is protected by a separate small cover.

Very fine full-width porches with balconies were to be seen at Horringer Road mill, Bury St Edmunds, Gt Barton mill and Stanton Chair mill which also boasted a copper roof. The head of Framsden mill was covered with canvas soaked in white lead paint before the last war while Skinner's mill, Stradbroke had the head covered with iron sheeting to keep out the wet. This mill was peculiar in having the ends of the crowntree projecting through the sides of the buck and protected by small lean-to covers. Eye mill and Fletcher's old open postmill at Wrentham had an excrescence on one side of the buck roof over the sack hoist, in the case of Eye having a door so that sacks could be hoisted up outside. Of course this could only have been achieved before the roundhouse was built.[16] Several mills including Darsham had a sack slide on the rear steps.

As has been said before interior details before the 1920s have seldom been recorded but of those mills examined a few oddities are worth mentioning. Westleton mill was unique in having the great spur wheel mounted *above* the wallower. At Gt Welnetham, Horham, Syleham and Westhall mills, due to lack of space, there was no hopper to the tail-stones, the bin spout having been directed to discharge straight into a large shoe. At Westhall this arrangement was also employed for the headstones. Several mills had an internal lining of tongued-and-grooved boards which provided a smooth, easily cleaned surface but at Darsham the upper floor of the buck was plastered inside.

Swilland post and steam mills

Wortham Ling post and steam mills

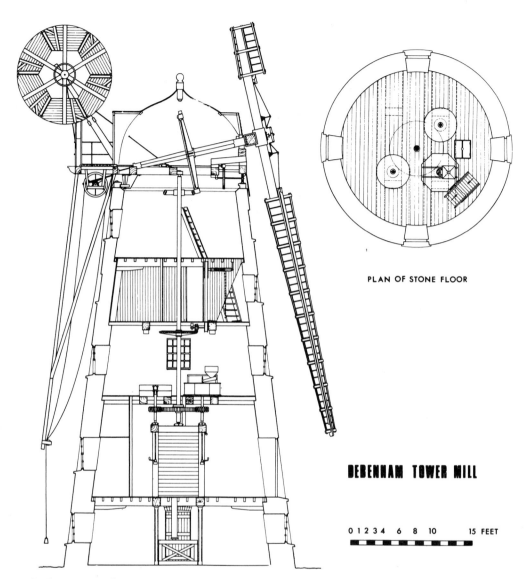

PLAN OF STONE FLOOR

DEBENHAM TOWER MILL

0 1 2 3 4   6   8   10   15 FEET

Debenham towermill

3

Towermills and Other Types

As mentioned in the previous chapter the towermill never ousted the 'old-fashioned' postmill in Suffolk, although some splendid examples were built here in the nineteenth century. Perhaps it should be explained that the towermill, as opposed to the postmill, has a stationary body containing the machinery and millstones, only the *cap*, containing the windshaft carrying the sails, revolving to face the wind. The smockmill is a variation and will be dealt with separately.

Unlike some towermills elsewhere, where local stone was available, those in Suffolk were almost invariably built of brick although Higham towermill, near Bury St Edmunds, was said to have been a combination of brick and stone. The most common brick was a warm red colour but 'Suffolk whites' were quite often used. Frequently, as with postmill roundhouses, the walls were tarred to keep out the wet and occasionally they were painted as at Bredfield which was dove grey and Burgh and Kelsale which were black and white. It is possible that in early days towers of clay lump and clunch (chalk) were built in Suffolk but, if so, none has survived.

The earliest reference to a towermill in England concerns one in Dover Castle in 1294–5.[1] No medieval reference, specifically to a towermill in Suffolk has come to light but a window of *c* 1470–80 in Stoke-by-Clare Church shows one and a fifteenth century wall painting, now indistinguishable, in Belton Church showed another together with a postmill.

The towermills, of which we have details, were all circular in plan with raked walls which varied from about 4 degrees off vertical at Chediston to about 10 degrees at Layham. Buxhall towermill, built on the foundations of a smockmill, has vertical walls to above third floor level whereas 'Lady Mill' at Oulton Broad gained its name from the waisted appearance which resulted when it was heightened by Robert Martin *c* 1860. Towers varied greatly in size, a small mill such as Gt Welnetham standing 28 ft 6 ins (8.7 m) to the curb while at the other extreme the aptly named 'High Mill', built in 1812 in Southtown, Gt Yarmouth (in Suffolk until 1891 when it was transferred to Norfolk) measured no less than

100 ft (30.5 m) to the top of the brickwork and was 46 ft (14 m) outside diameter at ground level. Incidentally, this mill had the windows arranged one under the other, a system not advocated on theoretical considerations as it must weaken the tower. However, the workmanship was such that the enormous structure, founded on an oak base supported by piles because of the marshy site, exhibits no visible cracks in extant photographs and was said to have been in perfect condition when demolished in 1905.

Internally the towermill is divided into storeys, the top floor being known as the *dust floor* and that next down usually the *bin floor* where the grain is stored before being ground. The stones might be situated on any floor from the first depending on the height of the tower. Beneath the *stone floor* is the *meal floor* where the meal is received from the stones. High Mill had no less than eleven floors but from four to six was usual. Ladders between floors are usually staggered in plan so that anyone losing his footing on the steps would not fall to the bottom of the mill. At 'Waterloo Mill', Bramfield, proper staircases were provided with elegant handrail and balusters.

External stages for access to the sails or for loading purposes were not the norm in Suffolk but several of the taller towers had stages, that at High Mill being situated at seventh floor level whilst on the last Haverhill mill there was a movable portion suspended from the main stage on chains.

Usually the most distinctive feature of any towermill is the cap. Unlike several other counties no particular cap shape may be called typical, the boat cap, common in the north-east corner of the country, being more representative of Norfolk. Of those mills of which we have photographs, it appears the most common cap shapes were the dome or round and the boat shape. Dome-shaped caps comprised slightly more than a third of the total and were mostly confined to the area which used to constitute West Suffolk. They were generally horizontally boarded although the boards were laid vertically on the annular-sailed mill at Haverhill.

The boat cap accounted for another third of the total and, with the exception of Gazeley and Redgrave, were all in what was East Suffolk. Ogee caps seem to have been the prerogative of Whitmore mills and again were confined to the eastern half of the county, with the exception of the larger towermill at Rattlesden which may not have been of Whitmore manufacture. These ogee caps, of which one example remains at Woodbridge, were shallower than those in Lincolnshire and were horizontally boarded. Conical or acorn-shaped caps were less common and predominated in the west, a notable exception being on the mill which stood until about the turn of the century in Church Road, Lowestoft. Hinderclay mill alone carried a cap shaped like the top of a postmill buck.

The size of most of these caps is unknown and in the case of High Mill must have been very large although perhaps not much bigger than on the fine mill at

Burgh towermill   *Layham towermill*

Buxhall which Mr Wailes measured at 17 ft 6 ins (5.34 m) diameter by 14 ft (4.27 m) high (inside dimensions). Caps, with the exception of the boat-shaped, were usually furnished with a finial but the famous High Mill was unique in carrying, at one time, a cage or cupola which may have been connected with the fact that the mill was used by mariners as a sea mark but it appears it was unlikely ever to have carried a navigational light.[2] The cage was in turn surmounted by a wooden weather vane in the form of a flame, the total height over this being no less than 132 ft (40.3 m). This vane was preserved after the mill was demolished but unfortunately was destroyed in a bombing raid during the last war.

Over a half of the boat-shaped caps had access galleries around them. These were usually of wood with iron handrails. Galleries were slightly less common on dome caps and apparently not fitted on any of the conical caps seen. Bardwell and Bramfield mills were also furnished with curved ladders which could be lashed to the finial and give access to the top of the cap for painting and repairs.

Caps were nearly always boarded and sometimes canvas-covered, Pakenham being the only Suffolk towermill known to have had a copper covered cap. This was removed and aluminium sheet substituted when the mill was restored. The cap gallery on this mill is also quite a recent addition and serves as a splendid viewing platform for the many visitors.

As far as is known the towermill curbs were generally of the *live* type, that is with

Preston towermill c. 1907

Metfield towermill

rollers fixed to the underside of the cap and running on an iron track packed up on top of the tower brickwork. On the annular-sailed mill at Haverhill these wheels, which were grooved, ran on a rail, thus helping to retain the cap radially or *centre* it although this task was performed here, as on other mills, by horizontal wheels attached to the cap frame and running on the inside face of the curb. Often the centering wheels ran under a step in the curb thus acting as *keeps* to prevent the cap from lifting. Tricker's mill at Woodbridge was very unusual as the centering wheels were arranged to run on the outside of the curb possibly as the result of a cap from another mill being fitted after the original one was blown off.

Buxhall mill boasted a further refinement in having an iron gutter fitted outside the curb to collect water from the cap and convey it to ground level by means of a downpipe on the outside of the tower.

Early towermills, like their postmill contemporaries, were winded by means of a tailpole braced to the cap and extending to near ground level. This arrangement is still common in Holland but has not survived on any corn towermill here although the towermill which stood until 1868 near Wickham Market watermill is said to have had a tailpole. The later method of turning the cap, by means of an endless chain over a wheel connected to a worm engaging with a gear rack at the curb, was also probably common at one time but only Gt Bradley mill is remembered with this feature. All the other towermills in Suffolk of which we have details were winded by a fantail with either six or eight blades, as with the postmills six-bladed *flys* being the more common.

In Suffolk the fly-frame was usually erected on the two *sheers* or main longitudinal cap beams which project through the rear of the cap. Access was provided by a door in the rear cap gable and often ladder rungs were nailed to one, or both of the vertical or raked fly-posts. The sheers often rotted where they emerged from the cap and at Barnham mill they were repaired with cast-iron extensions.

Various methods of transmitting the drive from the fly to a gear rack at the curb were used. The most usual arrangement was for the rack to be on the top, outside the roller track with a spur pinion meshing with it. This was the method favoured by Whitmores. At Tricker's mill, Woodbridge, the tower of which still stands, the rack is mounted inside the roller track and faces inwards. Gazeley mill was unusual in having an iron worm meshing with the rack which was mounted outside the roller track facing outwards.

Early towermills of course carried common sails with stocks mortised through a wooden windshaft. Although found quite late on drainage mills (see chapter 5) the only corn towermills remembered with four common sails were at Ufford and the little mill previously alluded to at Wickham Market. When this was pulled down the bricks were used for the Whitmore and Binyon roller-mill building. An old photograph shows the squat little mill on Stowupland Green to have had two common and two double shuttered sails as had Gislingham towermill prior to 1925 when a pair of patents from Hoxne postmill replaced the common sails. A towermill with spring sails was advertised for sale in Woodbridge Road Ipswich in 1836[3] but these sails were quite rare, latterly the only examples known of towermills with them being at Ilketshall St Lawrence, where the sails were double-sided and regulated with half-elliptic springs, and at Kersey where the spring sails were eventually blown off and replaced with patents from a postmill at Creeting St Mary.

Patent sails were typically double-sided and rotated anti-clockwise when viewed from the front; in fact no illustration has come to light which shows a 'left-handed' towermill. Sails were usually of eight or nine bays length with three shutters to each bay although several powerful towermills such as Beccles, Bungay, Debenham and Preston had ten-bay sails. Buxhall mill was exceptional in having eleven-bay sails spanning 80 ft (24.4 m) and equipped with Catchpole's 'skyscrapers'. High Mill, Southtown had sails reputedly of 84 ft (25.6 m) span but nevertheless were of only ten bays each.

The only other towermill fitted with Catchpole's air brakes was the larger one at Rattlesden, demolished *c* 1918.

One multi-sailed towermill is known to have stood in Suffolk by the Nowton Road on the outskirts of Bury St Edmunds. Built in 1836 this was fitted with six double-sided patent sails, dome-shaped cap and eight-bladed fly. It was last worked by Samuel Scarfe shortly before the turn of the century but no photograph of it is known to have survived.

The majority of towermills appear to have had a rack, at the rear of the striking rod, meshing with a pinion on the same spindle as a chain wheel just as on most postmills. The weight chain usually hung down to ground level and it was not unusual for a long, braced pole to project down from the back of the fly frame to guide the chain and keep it clear of the mill tower.

Of the four corn mills known to have been fitted with annular or circular sails, two stood in Suffolk. These were the smock mill at Boxford and the well known towermill which graced Haverhill until 1942. Mr Richard Ruffle had this mill built about 1855 on the site of his old postmill which he had unsuccessfully converted to a composite mill a few years previously. The annular sail was originally the idea of an Essex miller, Henry Chopping who fitted one to his postmill at Roxwell, near Chelmsford.

Mr Ruffle, who had a mechanical turn of mind, heard of the invention and obtained a drawing illustrating it from Chopping. From this he first made a working model, and being pleased with the result, proceeded to have a full-size version manufactured and fitted to his new towermill.[4]

The sail was either 48 ft (14.63 m) or 50 ft (15.24 m) in diameter and had 120 shutters, each tapering from $12\frac{1}{2}$ ins (318 mm) to $14\frac{1}{2}$ in (368 mm) by 5 ft

High Mill, Southtown

Haverhill towermill with annular sail c. 1930

(1.52 m) long with wooden frames, canvas covered, and mounted between two angle-iron rings. These were carried on eight wooden arms bolted into the channel-section arms of an iron 'cross' fixed to the end of the windshaft. The shutters were operated by four rods running along alternate arms to bell-cranks fitted to the arms at the radial centreline of the shutters. These rods were actuated by the striking rod in the normal manner through a spider coupling and 'triangles'. A circumferential striking *ring* was connected to the outer bell-cranks and also to the shutters by a lever mounted centrally on each. The striking mechanism was, at one time, regulated by a large ball-governor in the cap. This fine mill, which drove four pairs of stones and an oat crusher, worked until sustaining damage in 1933 and was substantially complete when demolished.

Apart from those constructed for drainage purposes, which will be discussed later, the vast majority of towermills were equipped with stones to grind wheat into flour, although many finished their working days milling cattle and pig feed. One towermill, whose stump still lingered in Victoria Road, Woodbridge, early this century, was built by Mr Lockwood, a local builder *c* 1825 to grind clinker for cement. It was equipped with granite millstones obtained from Aberdeen, these presumably being 'edge runners'. The mill suffered gale damage in 1841 and probably ceased work by wind at that date. The 1882, 6 inch OS map shows, for the first time a windmill, of unknown type, situated in a brickworks on the west

Tricker's mill, Woodbridge; great spurwheel

Buttrum's mill, Woodbridge; striking gear

side of Lowestoft. It seems probable that this was erected for the purpose of crushing brick-earth.

A sale notice of 1804[5] referred to 'a small Drug Windmill with iron cylinders' situated near a postmill on the Woodbridge Road, Ipswich but it is not clear whether this was a towermill or another type. It would have been used for grinding constituents for medicines but the type of mechanism employed is open to conjecture.

Early corn towermills contained a single pair of millstones situated centrally and driven directly by a vertical *upright shaft* which carried the wallower at its upper end meshing with the head-wheel. This rather primitive layout is to be seen elsewhere to this day but was superseded in Suffolk by the more modern arrangement of positioning the stones around the upright shaft and driving them by means of a 'great spur wheel' and stone nuts.

This method allowed several pairs of stones to be installed, depending on the size of the mill, two or three being the most common number. At Pakenham the third pair of stones, of only 3 ft (914 mm) diameter, used to be over-driven from an internal gear on the great spur wheel. Some powerfull mills such as Beccles, Burgh, Buttrums Mill, Woodbridge and High Mill, Southtown carried four pairs of stones whilst Buxhall had five. Of course these would not all be driven at once although it was not unknown for a big towermill to turn four if required in a strong wind.

In towermills *underdrift* stones were more common that *overdrift*, Whitmores favouring the former arrangement. From evidence available before the last war, when Stanley Freese and others examined those mills remaining, it appears that a separate governor for each pair of stones was almost always the rule although one governor controlling two pairs of stones is to be observed at Buttrums Mill, Woodbridge. The most common mode of operation was by belt-drive from the stone-spindles. However, at Pakenham chain-driven governors are fitted. Most governors were of the two-armed type although one of the two pairs in Bramfield Mill had four arms and was of large dimensions.

The only photograph to exist showing a towermill here with wooden windshaft is of the previously mentioned mill on Stowupland Green but iron postmill windshafts were to be found at Lound and Tricker's Mill, Woodbridge, while two-piece shafts, a type common in Norfolk, were fitted at Bardwell, Barnham, Bramfield and Lound mills.[6]

Similarly no early brakewheel, with evidence of having been mounted originally with compass-arms, was to be found on any of the towermills examined. Although several mills had wooden brakewheels with either mortised wooden cogs or bolted-on iron cog segments towermill brakewheels in general demonstrated a later technology than their postmill counterparts. This indeed could be said of the majority of towermill machinery, a case in point being the provision of iron cranes to lift and turn the runner stones for dressing in several mills. Such a crane was fitted in the Haverhill annular-sailed mill and in the Whitmore-built mills at Debenham and Rattlesden. In addition to these we know Whitmores built the towermills at Burgh, Framlingham, Kelsale and Woodbridge. It is probable that Hasketon, Bramford Road Ipswich, and the second, larger towermill at Rattlesden were also erected by Whitmores while doubtless there were others of which no photograph has survived to give us the clue.

Whitmore mills were very distinctive and Buttrum's Mill at Woodbridge, the only nearly complete survivor, may be taken as fairly typical. The gallery to the ogee-shaped cap was furnished with an attractive fancy iron handrail—that in wood being a modern replacement—and Burgh mill was similarly equipped. The gallery handrails on Debenham, Framlingham and Kelsale were of a much plainer design. Buttrum's mill was built during 1816–17 whereas Debenham dated from 1839, Framlingham from 1843, Burgh from 1842 and Kelsale as late as 1856. Rattlesden mill of *c* 1850, which was much smaller than any of these others, had no gallery to the cap and neither had Hasketon while it is uncertain whether or not the larger mill at Rattlesden was so equipped.

These mills carried patent sails and six-bladed flys and the tower at Kelsale has iron window frames. Sizes varied considerably, Rattlesden standing only 47 ft 6 ins (14.5 m) over the cap, 14 ft (4.27 m) inside diameter at the base and 6 ft 6 ins (1.98 m) at the curb. Buttrum's mill is quite slender at 20 ft 6 ins (6.25 m) base inside diameter and 11 ft (3.36 m) at the curb and, with six floors, looks tall although measuring only 48 ft (14.64 m) over the brickwork. Framlingham had six floors and measured 23 ft 6 ins (7.17 m) outside diameter at the base. Kelsale with seven floors measures 55 ft 2 ins (16.8 m) to the top of the brickwork and again is slender at 21 ft 6 ins (6.56 m) base inside diameter and only 10 ft 10 ins (3.3 m) at the curb. Debenham was a large mill tapering from 23 ft (7 m) inside diameter at the base to 14 ft (4.27 m) at the curb and standing more than 57 ft (17.4 m) high over the cap finial. Burgh was the largest Whitmore mill measured. With seven floors like Kelsale the empty brick tower still stands 56 ft 7 ins (17.27 m) high and is 23 ft 2 ins (7.06 m) inside diameter at the base where the walls are 30 ins (762 mm) thick. The inside diameter of the brickwork at the curb is 13 ft 11 ins (4.24 m).

At Framlingham and Kelsale there were adjacent steam mills whereas Burgh and Buttrum's mill have adjoining granary buildings. Debenham and Kelsale each drove three pairs of stones by wind, Debenham having a fourth pair on the ground floor engine driven. Burgh and Buttrum's mill each had four pairs wind driven, Burgh also having an E. R. & F. Turner 8 h.p. oil engine in the adjoining building with belt drive to a pulley on the third floor which carried the stones and Buttrum's also having provision for an engine drive.

Debenham and Rattlesden alone bore tailpole guides for the striking chains. At

Lound towermill in 1934

Debenham the striking rod was connected to a single rack in the usual manner but at Buttrum's mill, Woodbridge the rod is connected to twin racks projecting forward within the cap and running on rollers while the striking chain was operated from inside the mill. This presumably was the arrangement in Burgh, Framlingham and Kelsale mills, none of which appears to have had an external purchase wheel. Debenham mill and Buttrum's contained another interesting feature in having a 'speaking tube' from top to bottom of the mill. In general sack-hoist drives were taken from a separate bevel gearwheel mounted on the upright shaft as at Bardwell, Blundeston, Debenham, Thelnetham and Buttrum's mill or from an inverted wooden friction rim mounted on the underside of the wallower as at Pakenham. A third method, employed at Haverhill and Tricker's mill, Woodbridge, was to drive from a bevel ring mounted on the great spur wheel, that on Haverhill being mounted underneath while Tricker's has the ring on top of the spur wheel.

It was common for towermills to contain belt-driven wire machines or bolters. Oat crushers, which are a comparatively modern machine, were to be found in quite a few mills and a 'smutter', used for removing a fungus called smut from wheat, was installed in the annular-sailed Haverhill mill. Tricker's mill at Woodbridge had suspended under the first floor a pair of reciprocating screens. These have had to be removed recently but are being preserved. At Burgh Castle mill the flour dresser was powered by an engine as it was said to be too erratic if wind driven.

Hinderclay mill contained a horizontal capstan, similar to that in Framsden postmill, for turning the stones.

Often, when an old postmill became ricketty and uneconomical to repair, the owner would have it pulled down and a 'modern' towermill erected on the same site. This was the case, as previously stated, at Haverhill and also at Buxhall where the postmill was succeeded by a smockmill prior to the towermill being built. Debenham towermill was also built on the site of a postmill which overturned when it was being heightened and Framlingham similarly replaced a postmill 'recently erected' in 1574 and burned in 1842.

Gazeley mill was built in 1844 by Mr William Death, whose father had for many years worked a postmill on an adjacent site. The mill was fitted with five pairs of stones, three pairs of which could be driven by an engine. In 1893, on the decease of Mr Death, the mill was purchased by Mr R. J. Harvey who had been tenant miller for a number of years. Mr Harvey, finding that the product of the existing plant could not compete with roller flour, decided to install a one-and-a-half sack roller plant supplied by Messrs E. R. & F. Turner of Ipswich. As he wished to keep the wind power at disposal for driving two pairs of stones for grist the space available for the roller plant was very limited but the installation was ingeniously arranged and, driven by the small Gippeswyk horizontal oil engine previously supplied by Turners in 1880 to drive the stones, performed to Mr Harvey's complete satisfaction.[7]

Waterloo Mill, Bramfield, was built on a mound previously occupied by a postmill which was advertised to be sold in 1802 and 1803. Hinderclay mill also superseded a postmill on the same site as did Lavenham, Lound and Stansfield mills. Hodskinson, on his map of 1783, shows a mill near or where Thelnetham mill was built in 1819. Burgh mill was erected in the same yard as an earlier small towermill whilst Messrs T & J Skoulding had the towermill put up in the same yard as their postmill at Kelsale. A postmill roundhouse used to stand close to Tricker's mill, Woodbridge, the circular foundations and pier bases still being visible when Stanley Freese visited the site in the 1930s. The mound on which previously stood a postmill was also to be seen close to Barnham towermill.

Sometimes when a mill sustained gale damage it would be reinstated with parts from another mill which had gone out of use. This occurred at Debenham mill which lost its cap during the first world war. In 1920 it was refurbished with sails, stocks, windshaft, brakewheel, brake and wallower from Preston towermill. However, the cap was rebuilt in the original Whitmore style.

After Buxhall mill was damaged in a storm in November 1929 the 'swing-pot' neck bearing and brass were removed and eventually sold to Mr John Bryant of Pakenham mill. At this time (1950) Amos Clarke was fitting a new weather beam at Pakenham and, as the old neck-brass housing had no provision for adjustment, replaced it with the self-aligning unit from Buxhall, which incidentally is still in use.

Towermills seem not to have been given affectionate names as frequently as postmills, although 'Tutelina Mill', Gt Welnetham[8] and 'Lady Mill' at Oulton Broad were exceptions. 'Waterloo Mill' Bramfield carried a wall stone bearing its name and the date, 1815, being, of course, the year of the famous battle. Framlingham towermill was called 'Victoria Mill' although the reason is not clear as the good Queen had been enthroned six years previously when the mill was built. Hitcham towermill or its predecessor is accorded the name 'Cross Mill' on Bryant's map of 1826; it stood on Cross Green. 'Pepper Mill' at Cockfield was almost certainly a corn mill; its name presumably derived from nearby Pepper Hall. The only other towermill which bore a distinctive name—as opposed to simply the miller's or owner's name—was 'Greencap Mill' which stood in Southtown, Gt Yarmouth until being burned in 1898. Like the nearby High Mill this was a very tall towermill, standing 92 ft (28.05 m) to the curb, and in view of its name may have carried a copper sheeted cap.

Several towermills, other than those already mentioned, were dated. Bardwell has the date 1823 carved on the sprattle beam and Barnham, built for the Duke of Grafton in 1821, bears a date stone. The tall towermill at Bungay, which is now a house, is dated 1830 and the tiny mill tower at Gt Welnetham bears the late date

1865. The stump of Metfield towermill carries no fewer than three tablets attesting to the date of building, August 5th 1839 and the names T. (or I) Chase, W. Booth and G. Godbold. Debenham, built in the same year carries the initials 'C.C.' for Claud Chevallier, of barley fame, who had it built. Stansfield mill is dated 1840 whilst Thelnetham mill, which was put up in 1819, has an iron windshaft cast by J. Aickman of Kings Lynn in 1832 and fitted on July 16th of that year.[9] Tricker's mill, Woodbridge has carved on a brick on the outside of the tower 'W(?) Mower Feby 2 1835' but the mill is known to have been standing in 1815. Preston mill bore a stone marked 'J. Edgar, Felsham 1846'.

Wickham Skeith was probably the last corn towermill built in the county *c* 1870 with the exception of the very late little mill at Cockfield, alluded to in Chapter 4, which bore the legend 'AM 1891'.

A smockmill is simply a towermill with a timber or smocked tower. It has been said to have derived its name from a fancied resemblance to the old countryman's smock garment. Smock mills were nearly as common as towermills in Suffolk in the nineteenth century but together with towermills accounted for only one third of the total number of windmills despite the fact that the smockmill like the postmill, is a predominantly wooden structure.

It is not certain when smockmills were introduced here but they have always been one of the principal types of drainage mill and may well have originated in Holland and been first erected in the country by Cornelius Vermuyden in the first half of the seventeenth century.

That they have in general survived less well that their often earlier postmill neighbours bears witness to a fundamental weakness in smockmill design. Being difficult to construct with circular walls the smockmill usually had eight flat sides each intersecting at a main support or *cant post*. As the smockmill body is stationary it must receive weather from all quarters and the inevitable result is ingress of water at these intersecting joints with consequent rotting of the cant posts leading eventually to distortion of the curb. Due to the batter of the walls another point of ingress is the window frames which cannot be recessed deeply as with a brick tower. In fact sloping walls which were usually clad in weather boarding could never be fully waterproof.

The only Suffolk smockmills known not to have been octagonal were Blythburgh (twelve sided) and Wangford and Wortham which had ten sides. The cant posts were seated on wooden sills which were laid on a brick base but this could vary in height considerably, from a few brick courses above ground as at Rushmere St Andrew and Westleton to as much as three storeys at the big Highfield Mill at Sudbury. This mill, with a further three floors in the smocked portion, drove four pairs of stones and must have been almost 70 ft (21.3 m) tall over the finial of its dome-shaped cap—nearly as tall as the finest remaining smockmill in England, at Cranbrook in Kent.

Bardwell towermill in 1911

Barnham towermill c. 1929

Bungay towermill

Westleton smockmill in 1899

The base of Highfield Mill, converted to a roomy house in 1927, has sloping walls but vertical walls were sometimes used and, in the west of the county, it was common to build vertically but to reduce the size of the base as it progressed upwards by stepping the walls in half the thickness of a brick every six to ten courses as can still be seen in the bases of Dalham and Shimpling mills. Drinkstone smockmill has a basement which was originally a two-pair horse mill.

Although horizontal boarding was the norm, some smockmills near the Cambridgeshire border followed the practice of that county in being clad in vertical boarding. This was the case at Dalham mill at one time and also at Kings Road, Bury St Edmunds and Newmarket whilst Gt Thurlow mill had vertical boards laid over the earlier horizontal boarding before it was restored. In East Suffolk, Blythburgh mill alone carried vertical boarding.

As well as being painted or tarred on the outside several smockmills were plastered inside. These included Dalham, Drinkstone, Freckenham, Gt Bricett and Wortham. As a further attempt at keeping out the wet Laxfield mill body was covered with iron sheeting as was the body and cap of Cransford mill after it was set up at Peasenhall, although it never carried sails here.

Unlike Kentish smockmills those in Suffolk, of which we have details, seldom had stages to the towers. This may be partly explained by the fact that spring sails were common in Kent whereas in Suffolk the patent sail became almost universal. However two of the largest smockmills, at Sudbury and Wangford, both with patent sails, had stages.

The most common cap shapes on smockmills were boat and conical in about equal numbers, as with towermills the conical shape being confined to the western half of the county, the only examples known in East Suffolk being at Alderton and Needham Market. Dome shaped caps, which were less common than on the towermills, also predominated in the west whilst boat caps were only found in East Suffolk with the sole exception at Freckenham. The conical cap on Barrow mill was copper-covered. A deep Kentish type cap was fitted to Cowlinge mill.

The conical cap of Gt Thurlow mill was plastered inside. Several of the conical caps, unlike their towermill counterparts, had galleries around them and these were also found with boat, dome and ogee shapes.

Again, *live curbs* were most common, but both Dalham and Gt Thurlow mills have 'shot curbs', that is with the rollers running between iron tracks on top of the curb and on the bottom of the cap. On Freckenham mill, wooden blocks were used instead of rollers to centre the cap.

The only smock cornmill noted with tailpole winding was that at Freckenham which was originally a drainage mill, although Gt Bricett mill had heavy beams projecting from the sides of the cap which may have originally supported a tailpole. Stanley Freese was told that the old smockmill which stood on Ward Green, Old Newton until *c* 1890 was tailpole-winded. Drinkstone mill was winded by a chain and wheel before Mr Clover's grandfather had a fly fitted. A wooden rack inside the curb was utilised originally but an iron rack meshing with an iron wormwheel was substituted when the fly was put up.

Fantail drives were generally similar to those on towermills with the rack outside the roller track and facing upwards. At Chattisham the rack was inside the track while at Dalham it is of wooden mortised cogs facing inwards and at Gt Thurlow the rack faces outwards. Usually an iron spur gear meshed with the rack but at Gt Thurlow an iron worm is used and at Wortham a wooden worm was fitted. Stanton smockmill had a split bevel drive from the fly turning two pinions meshing with the rack.

Alderton mill had a wooden rack facing upwards and arranged outside the curb in the usual manner with iron drive pinion. The fan drive was taken through the usual bevels to turn it through ninety degrees and then to an iron worm driving a wormwheel on the final pinion shaft. A wooden chainwheel for hand operation from the ground was also provided on the shaft carrying the worm. Of course it was usual for alternative hand operation to be provided in case of tail-winding.

Common sails were to be found latterly on several corn smockmills but only at Flowton, pulled down early this century, and Brettenham were four cloth sails remembered, the latter carried on a mortised wooden windshaft. Later at Brettenham one pair were replaced with single shuttered spring sails.

Drinkstone smock also had two cloth sails and two spring whilst Old Newton mill was said to have had two commons and two patents. Cowlinge and Freckenham mills were 'left handed' and both bore two common and two patent

Crowfield smockmill; drive to the stones

Dalham smockmill ; hurst frame

sails. The only smock noted with four spring sails was at Edwardstone.

Of those mills with patent sails Barrow, Fornham St Martin, Gt Thurlow and Newmarket were left handed. Barrow and Fornham mills were remarkably similar in appearance and were doubtless the product of the same millwright.

As with the other types of mill the sail span varied considerably, and although precise measurements are not known, the sails on Bradfield St George, Sudbury and Wangford mills, with ten bays of three shutters, were the largest noted and compare with those on all but the biggest towermills. A smockmill of seven floors, advertised for sail in Bungay in 1830, was described as having 'patent sails with eleven yards of vane'[10] meaning, presumably, eleven bays of three shutters per sail.

Of multi-sailers we have but scanty references to one. This is the mill whose base still stands at Occold where it carried the usual four double-shuttered patents. It had been moved from Eye where it was said at one time to have had six common sails.

The annular-sailed smockmill at Boxford has already been mentioned. This mill is said to have been built in 1841 although a mill on this site is shown on earlier maps. In 1861 it was fitted with an annular sail by Alfred Clubb, a millwright from Colchester. He examined the Haverhill mill sail but was informed he must not infringe Henry Chopping's patent which related to the mode of striking gear. It is not clear, from the sole extant photograph, how the striking of the shutters was effected. The sail originally carried two rings of shutters but proved unmanageable in heavy weather so the inner set was removed and four short patent outriggers were added on alternate sail arms. These were of three bays of three shutters each and were said to have contributed to steadier running.

Mr E. Gowing, who worked in the mill, stated that the sail was effective, turning in a light wind and driving three pairs of stones if required. On 'Black Tuesday', twenty years after being fitted, the annular sail was smashed when the sockets of the iron cross fractured. The owner decided against having the sail repaired and employed Collins of Melton to fit four ordinary patent sails of ten bays with the normal canister windshaft end. Whether an entirely new windshaft was used is not certain. However the mill did not work for many more years, as it was out of use when pulled down in 1901.

No smockmill was fitted with Catchpole's 'skyscrapers' as far as we know.

Alderton mill was unusual in having twin racks and pinions outside the cap for 'striking' the sails.

Boxford, Bradfield St George, Freckenham, Gt and Lt Thurlow and Newmarket mills, all in the west of the county, had rocking levers in place of a chainwheel for striking the sails, Gt Thurlow also having a safety catch to prevent the shutters from closing if the mill were tail-winded.

A tailpole guide for the striking chains was quite common with boat shaped caps and was also fitted on the ogee-capped mill at Laxfield which is thought to have been built by Whitmores. The other 'Whitmore-looking' smockmill, at Westleton, did not have this feature but had what was either an external brake lever or a striking gear rocking lever controlled by a rope hanging to the ground.

Only one instance of a smockmill, other than a drainage mill, not being used exclusively for corn or grist grinding has come to my notice. This concerned the large, ten-sided Wangford mill which, although latterly fitted out with three pairs of stones, was built as a sawmill in the Earl of Stradbroke's estate and in the 1860s apparently operated both milling and sawing machinery. The mill was burnt while working on 7 August 1928, a sequence of photographs being taken of the event by a local resident.

Like Freckenham the little smockmill at Crowfield was brought from the marshes by the grandfather of the present owner Mr Gibbons. It is said to have originally stood near Gt Yarmouth and at its present site is equipped with two pairs of underdriven stones.

Several one-pair mills have been recorded including the tiny converted marshmill whose travellings are described in chapter 4. This mill had a pair of 3 ft 4 in (1.01 m) stones whereas another one-pair mill, at Kettleburgh, had stones of 4 ft 4 ins (1.32 m) diameter, the runner of which went to Parham postmill after the smock went out of use in the 1870s. Two or three pairs of stones were again the most common number but Bradfield St George and Highfield Mill, Sudbury had four pairs.

Over and under-driven stones seem to have gained about equal acceptance but a peculiarity confined to smock towers was the mounting of the stones on a *hurst frame*, as in a water mill. The mills noted with this feature were at Alderton, Boxford, Brettenham, Dalham, Drinkstone and Shimpling. The floor carrying the hurst was usually supported on the brickwork of the base but this was not the case at Brettenham and Drinkstone which were boarded down almost to the ground. It appears, that with this arrangement, underdriven stones were usually employed but in Alderton mill they were overdriven by wind although a separate drive from a steam engine drove the stone spindles from below. At one time the drive may have been arranged differently as an early photograph shows a power-pulley on the outside at second floor level whereas, in later years, the pulley was mounted just above the top of the brickwork, a floor lower. By then the mill had also been re-boarded and the position of some of the windows altered.

Governor drives followed towermill practice, the only peculiarities noted being at Gt Bricett where a spur wheel drive was taken from the bottom of the upright shaft, at Gt Thurlow which had a very unusual arrangement with one governor mounted above the underdrift stones on an extension to the damsel and at Dalham where the governors were belt driven from the damsel shafts.

Several wooden windshafts were still to be found in smockmills around the

Rushmere St Andrew smockmill in 1924   *Blythburgh smockmill in 1936*

turn of the century. The all-wooden shaft at Brettenham was eventually replaced by a 'standard' iron shaft, with cored hole for a striking rod if required, cast at Stowmarket. Drinkstone mill also had an all wooden shaft whereas at Gt Bricett, the wooden windshaft, bought at a sale for £2 in 1891, was fitted with an iron canister. This shaft remained in the mill until it was demolished in 1954. Dalham mill has an iron three-piece postmill windshaft with mountings for the brakewheel close behind the neck journal. Two-piece shafts were to be found in Rushmere St Andrew and Shadingfield smockmills.

Dalham mill has a brakewheel with compass-arm sockets, a feature which was also to be found at Gt Bricett. In contrast, Chattisham mill, of much later date, had a brakewheel entirely of iron. Alderton mill was notable in having a brakewheel with only forty-two cogs, the wheel diameter being 6 ft 8 ins (2.03 m).

Wallowers latterly were most commonly of iron although several wooden examples have been noted. At Freckenham a clasp-arm *trundle wheel* with upright staves, accorded further evidence of the mill's origin on the marshes.

Gt Bricett mill, which was built on the site of an old postmill in 1851 and damaged by the Colchester earthquake of 1884, contained the wooden postmill windshaft re-used as the upright shaft and one of the postmill gear-wheels utilised as the wallower.

From the above it will be apparent that the technology typified by smockmills in Suffolk was perhaps a little less advanced than in towermills here. At Dalham there is a horizontal wooden bollard for stone turning, whilst at Gt Thurlow there is a similar device but the only iron stone-crane recorded was in Chattisham mill.

Sack hoist drives in smockmills were similar to those in the towermills. Again a common method was to drive from a separate bevel gear on the upright shaft as at Alderton, Dalham, Palgrave, Peasenhall and Wortham. The drive at Wortham mill was from a compass-arm wheel fitted to the wooden section of the upright shaft. This presumably was from the original mill built in 1700 on a nearby site and almost entirely rebuilt *c* 1882 after being badly damaged in a gale. The other common method of driving from a friction rim under the wallower was employed at Bradfield St George, Drinkstone, Freckenham, Gt Bricett, Gt Thurlow and Shadingfield mills amongst others. In Wangford mill the sack-hoist was driven by an inverted gear on the underside of the great spur wheel.

Smockmills, although generally not as large and roomy as the brick towers, usually managed to accommodate at least one auxiliary machine, as at Drinkstone which had a bolter and Freckenham where this was situated on the ground floor and powered, via the usual belt drive, from a wooden crown wheel on the upright shaft above. Gt Thurlow mill contained a jumper at one time, to separate bran from middlings, as well as an oat crusher. At Alderton the oat crusher drive was from the same crown wheel which operated the sack hoist. Chattisham and Wangford mills had grindstones whilst at Brettenham and Bradfield St George inverted wooden face gears were bolted to the underside of the great spur wheel to drive machines which had vanished before the mills were examined. At Gt Bricett a similarly positioned iron bevel ring was used for the same purpose.

Many of the smockmills boasted auxiliary power in the form of a portable or stationary steam engine or sometimes an oil engine, in either case driving the mill machinery through a belt pulley on the outside of the tower. Brettenham mill utilised a portable engine which was kept in a little wooden shed but a more usual arrangement was to house a stationary engine nearby, the belt drive at Chattsiham being enclosed in an inclined wooden case as was done at Bungay towermill. Barking mill, near Needham Market, boasted an early Hornsby oil engine of pre-1895 date.

When Cransford smockmill was moved to Peasenhall it was not refitted with sails but powered only by a steam engine which also drove machines in the adjacent modern mill building.

Latterly several mills gave up working by wind but did useful work for years using auxiliary power. Chattisham mill, which lost its sail shutters *c* 1919 was worked by steam for a few more years. At Drinkstone, where the sails were removed from the smockmill about the turn of the century, Mr Clover continued

Brettenham smockmill

Drinkstone smockmill

work with an oil engine for many years as well as using the postmill by wind. Gt Bricett was worked for thirty-six years by an oil engine after the sails were removed in 1912. Laxfield mill ceased working by windpower in 1910 but was still power-driven thirty years later.

Smockmills also replaced old postmills on the same site, as has already been remarked at Boxford, Buxhall and Gt Bricett. Brettenham mill, dated 1804, took the place of a postmill shown on Hodskinson's map. Occold mill, thought to have come from Eye, presumably took the place of a mill shown on maps of 1826 and 1837. Gt Thurlow mill was said by the late owner, Mr Collis, to have superseded an earlier postmill and Little Thurlow did likewise. Westleton smock probably replaced an earlier mill shown by Hodskinson and Chattisham mill was either a rebuild or a replacement for a smockmill shown on a view of 1845 by Henry Davy, a local engraver.

The only colour peculiarities noted were at Rushmere St Andrew with its green fly and Shadingfield which had red sails. Today the conservationists would probably frown at such eccentricities but when windmills were common the odd splash of colour must have been a relief from severe black and white and made these mills look quite distinctive.

The earliest dated smockmill which stood recently enough to be recorded is Shimpling which bears the date 1792 three times with the appended initials VH, SA and SW. Brettenham had the date of building, 1804, carved on the sprattle beam whilst Palgrave mill carried the date 1803, in this instance being the date of rebuilding. At Gt Thurlow, the date of its removal—1807—is carved on a door post while its neighbour at Little Thurlow bears the inscription 'GB 1865'. On the ground floor of Freckenham mill, demolished in 1967, was to be found an inscription which read:

'THE FIRST GRIST GROUND AT THIS MILL WAS (BY) MR INO NORMAN, FRECKENHAM, JUNE 30TH, 1824'

The windshaft in Stanton mill carried the maker's name 'J. AICKMAN LYNN 1830'. This shaft was originally in Deopham mill, Norfolk.

An interesting fact concerning Alderton mill was the provision of a sliding shutter near the top of the tower which covered an opening in which used to be placed a signal light for the benefit of smugglers, of whom there once were quite a few operating on the Suffolk coast.

Before leaving smockmills mention should be made of one curious fellow, which although a working mill was really little more than a large model. This stood in the village of Grundisburgh where it was put up by a builder, by the name of Clarke, in about 1890. The mill which stood about 25 ft (7.63 m) high over the 'postmill buck top' shaped cap carried patent sails operated by wooden 'triangles' and 'cross'. A wooden windshaft carried a clasp-arm brakewheel

Rattlesden tower and smock mills

Wortham smockmill in 1937

Wangford smockmill

55

meshing with a wooden wallower on a slender iron upright shaft. One pair of 1 ft 6 ins (457 mm) diameter stones were underdriven on the second floor via an iron spur and nut. A small pair of lead-weighted governors were belt driven from the stone spindle and the set-up was reputed to grind very well. A chaff cutter on the first floor was belt driven from a layshaft under the bin floor. The little mill was winded by a braced tailpole but for the sake of appearance, presumably, a rather nasty looking dummy fly was provided.

This curiosity, built and worked as a hobby, was in working order in 1929 but had gone ten years later.

Mention has been made of a *composite* mill at Haverhill. A composite mill was usually constructed from the buck of an old postmill which had an ailing post. A short parallel tower or roundhouse would be constructed and the buck placed on top to rotate on rollers on the tower curb. Such a mill stood at Little Laver in Essex until 1964.

It appears that the fly was usually mounted on the buck roof and a ladder provided within the tower or roundhouse to gain access to the buck.

In 1803 were advertised two postmills within a hundred yards of each other at Halesworth.[11] At some later date the more easterly of the pair was converted to a composite mill, allegedly with patent sails and the fly on the roof. A steam auxiliary engine was later added and the mill stood until the early part of this century—several years after the demise of its close neighbour.

At Rishangles, north of Debenham, Hodskinson's map shows a mill to which was appended the name 'Wrights Mill' on Bryant's map. This was probably the mill shattered on 13 June 1826.[12] It may be that after sustaining severe gale damage the mill was rebuilt as a composite but it is uncertain whether this type of mill was constructed this early in the nineteenth century.

The two known surviving photographs show it to have had a two storey *roundhouse* with reinforcing bands attesting to a weakness in the brickwork. A conical roof with boarded petticoat encircled the curb. The six-bladed roof fan drove a vertical shaft on the rear face of the buck to a pair of bevels at the level of the curb. Presumably the drive was taken to a rack at the curb exactly as on a towermill. An internal revolving ladder was attached to the underside of the buck within the roundhouse.

The mill, which drove two pairs of stones with the old 'head and tail' arrangement, was burned in 1903 as described in chapter 4.

The only other composite mill known to have stood in Suffolk, and the only one which survived late enough to be examined and some of the details recorded, was at Monk Soham north east of Debenham.

A mill is first shown at Monk Soham on the 1837 OS map but at a site a little over a quarter of a mile south of its final position. The date of removal is unknown but is thought to have been fairly soon after the Ordnance surveyors recorded its

Rishangles composite mill in 1898

Grundisburgh model smockmill in 1938

earlier location. At its later site the low red brick *roundhouse* contained no piers, only lozenge-shaped projections to support the corners of a square frame on which was mounted a circular wooden curb with an inserted iron track on which ran the nine travelling wheels. Two of these were positioned under the head and the others equally spaced around the underframe of the buck. A hexagonal iron rod framework carried six centering wheels, that at the tail being larger than the others.

The tall, narrow buck was lightly framed and no braces were provided to receive the strain of suspension from a crown tree. It is believed that the mill was built from scratch as a composite as there was no evidence of it having had a trestle and crown tree and if so may well have been unique in being constructed thus. The projecting skirt so resembled the shallow roof of a roundhouse, there being no vertical boards around the periphery, that the casual viewer might be forgiven for thinking it was an ordinary postmill.

The mill was unusual in several other respects. The all wooden windshaft appears to have been a replacement, coming from Bedfield postmill when that was pulled down early this century. Bedfield mill was larger so the head was cut off the windshaft and the neck trimmed and mortised for the stocks. A new neck was turned on it and the brakewheel secured to the shaft with four iron plates. The four common sails turned clockwise.

Two pairs of stones, 3 ft 8 ins (1.12 m) and 4 ft (1.22 m) diameter, were overdriven in the head by wooden nuts, the remainder of the machinery being of iron.

The six-bladed fly and unusual drive arrangement was taken from the second postmill at Framsden as described in the previous chapter. The arrangement was never satisfactory as the worm persisted in binding up as apparently it had done at Framsden.

The mill is believed to have gone out of use by the beginning of the First World War and latterly only carried two sail frames. In 1935 Jesse Wightman removed the stones for the owner, Robert Nestling, and in November 1937 the mill was pulled over by traction engine, the roundhouse remaining virtually undamaged but being subsequently demolished.

Monk Soham composite mill; tram wheels

Monk Soham composite mill; underside of buck

William Goodchild, miller at Stoke, Ipswich

4

The Miller and the Millwright

The custom of milling *soke* or manorial privilege has been adequately dealt with elsewhere.[1] In Ipswich during the reign of Edward IV, it was decreed that 'All the inhabitants of the Towne shall grinde their corne at the Towne mills under forfature of halfe a Bushell of Corne for every bushell ground elsewhere.'[2] The matter of a windmill belonging to the abbey at Bury St Edmunds has been mentioned previously and it is probable that a foundation as important as was that at Bury owned more than one mill by the 13th or 14th century. Leiston Abbey owned at least one windmill and the old postmill on Rougham Common was built on glebe land and ground for the poor. In the parish of Barham, near Claydon, a windmill belonged to the House of Industry nearby[3] as did others at Melton and Onehouse.[4] The millers who worked there and the many manorial windmills in the county were of course tenants and right up to the twentieth century many millers leased their mills from the owners although sometimes tenant millers managed to purchase the mills in which they worked, occasionally forming partnerships to do this.

It has been said[5] that, in early days, the miller was not considered as being inherently honest and it may well be that the old system of taking a *toll* (usually a sixteenth part) of the grist ground at the Lord of the Manor's mill encouraged many millers to take more than their lawful share. It is apparent that this situation obtained in Ipswich towards the close of the thirteenth century when an order was made 'that millers taking more than their just toll; for the first offence shall be put into the pillory from one of the clock to three; and for the second offence, from one to nine of the clock; and for the third offence, from one to nine, and forejure the trade'.[2]

That this situation still obtained over 500 years later is evidenced by the fact that George Willis, a miller of Boxford, was convicted of taking toll as well as a money payment for which a penalty of 20s plus costs was exacted.[6] However the paucity of this sort of reference points to the fact that millers were inherently no more dishonest than men of most other callings.

A mill would often remain in the ownership of one family for many years; Drinkstone postmill was owned by Mr Wilfred Clover, having been in his family for over two centuries. Thorndon postmill belonged to the Lock family for four generations (all with the Christian name Nathan), whilst the mill on Broad Green, Wetheringsett was in the Aldred family for many years; and Bedingfield mill was owned and worked by several generations of the Cracknell family, all christened Syer.

Members of milling families often owned several mills in a neighbourhood, for example the Clovers having had milling interests in the 1890s at Buxhall, Colchester, Layham, Nedging, Leavenheath, Stoke-by-Nayland and Sudbury as well as Drinkstone. Other well-known milling families in Suffolk included the Aldridges of Walpole and later St Michael South Elmham, the Bryants latterly at Pakenham and Stanton mills, the Coles of Peasenhall and Stradbroke, the Elmers of Chelmondiston, Woolpit and elsewhere, and the Pykes of Woolpit and later Preston and Gedding where a branch of the family retained the earlier spelling *Pike*.

Quite often millers also farmed as did some of the Aldreds, Aldridges, Bryants, Clovers and Locks amongst others. Some millers combined less likely occupations. For example at Icklingham in 1844 James Benstead was the local schoolmaster as well as being a miller but whether anyone could manage two such demanding professions seems unlikely. However he was not alone in combining these callings as at the same time William Nichols was doing likewise at Barham and Thomas Bruster at Stoke-by-Clare. William Rowe, miller at Redlingfield at this time, was also running a beer house while at Oulton, John Knight was manufacturing cement as well as grinding corn.

Quite frequently millers were also corn or flour merchants, bakers or maltsters and several were coal merchants.

In 1891 at Ewardstone the miller, Harry Baker lived up to his name baking bread, as well as keeping a shop and acting as local carrier and postmaster. At this time the Orford miller, George Leach, was also the village postmaster. William Clement Fuller, miller and farmer at Wickambrook, carried out the duties of assistant overseer and clerk to the Wickambrook, Lidgate and Stradishall School Board while Henry Barrell at Huntingfield acted as district assessor and tax collector.

The millers' life was a hard one; before the advent of steam engines to provide an alternative power source he had to work long hours when the wind blew, as tomorrow he might be becalmed. Or again his friend the wind might blow too hard and become a fierce adversary, overturning his mill—if it were a postmill— as happened at Boxford on a March night in 1604 when the fall resulted in one fatal and two serious casualties.[7]

In 1795 a windmill on Bishops Hill, Ipswich was demolished by the wind

Wilfred Clover and his father at Drinkstone mill in 1938

Miller's wagon at Wortham in 1936

whilst the sails of the two postmills on Stoke Hill in the same town were carried away. It must have been a tremendous gale as it also blew down a newly erected windmill at Cornard and removed the cap and sails of another at Ballingdon.[8] A week later, in another storm, windmills at Badingham and Lavenham were destroyed, the owner of the latter being killed.[9]

In the winter of 1799 a gale split the post of the windmill at Trimley, which was destroyed, but a boy, inside at the time, was fortunate to escape unscathed.[10] An incident at Laxfield twenty-four years later is worth recounting in full:

'On Wednesday se 'nnight. . . . (Evening) amidst a tremendous storm of snow and hail a sudden hurrican arose, when a post windmill at Laxfield was blown down and dashed to atoms, and to the astonishment of all who witnessed the amazing and tremendous crash, Mr Henry Garrard had stopped the mill, and being upon the threshold of the mill in the act of descending the stairs, which instantaneously broke, and the mill run upon her peers (sic) and fell, and Mr G. within the midst of her ruins, but the door being left open (outward) and falling exactly perpendicular, and the bearers of the pentice sticking into the ground and becoming shored with the door, which prevented the tail end of the mill falling flat on the ground, in which small space Mr G. made his providential escape without sustaining the least bodily harm, being thrown under the door post, which space was not more than $2\frac{1}{2}$ ft from the ground; at the same time the wheat, barley, beans and weights, which were in the mill fell in the space of the doorway where Mr G. was standing one moment before.'[11]

Many other instances of gale damage could be cited but perhaps the worst was on Friday 26 November 1703 when more than 400 windmills in England were said to have been 'overset, broken or fired'.[12]

In more recent times 18 January 1881 became known as 'Black Tuesday' because of the severity of the weather in which heavy snowfall accompanied easterly gale-force winds resulting in extensive damage throughout the eastern counties. The late Mr Harry Elmer of Woolpit remembered the occasion many years afterwards:

'I was grinding in my windmill during the great blizzard of Jan. 18th 1881. The gale was nothing so strong as I have known, but the snow never ceased all the day. It drifted in our lane leading to the mill so that the snow had to be cut away before we could get our carts up, and every sack which was pulled up from the roundhouse was covered with snow which had drifted under the mill.'[13]

During the day Mr Aldred's mill at Wetheringsett was blown down when the post broke at the shoulder. It was rebuilt in 1882 with the roundhouse heightened and this still stands. A postmill at Hollesley lost its sails on the same day and the smockmill at Boxford had its annular sail smashed. Coddenham postmill also suffered some damage and another postmill at Redlingfield was demolished while the cap and sails were blown off Wortham smockmill.

An interesting account of gale damage and the ingenious solution to the resulting problem was recounted to me by Mr Claude Aldridge of Barningham Mills. It was while he had St Michael South Elmham postmill that the windshaft lifted in a gale and came right out of the swing-pot which tilted so that when the shaft dropped it landed on the edge of the iron neck bearing housing. He continued working the mill, unaware of what had happened, until, late in the day, he noticed a quantity of iron filings and decided to investigate. He called in a millwright who realised what had happened and told Mr Aldridge to drill into the windshaft and ascertain whether a minimum of 2 ins (51 mm) of iron was left between the bottom of the groove, worn in the shaft, and the hole for the striking rod. This he did and finding nearly $2\frac{1}{2}$ ins (63 mm) of metal left, the millwright made a stepped brass, fitting it to suit the profile of the groove, and it worked perfectly.

Another danger confronting the windmiller was that of being 'tail-winded'. It is not uncommon, before a storm, for the wind to die away and then suddenly freshen again but from the opposite direction to that at which it last blew. The fantail-winded mill was as vulnerable in this situation as its tailpole-winded neighbour for the fly could not respond to a wind dead on the tail. If the miller was quick enough he could uncouple the drive from the fly and turn the mill round to face the wind again by means of the hand-cranking mechanism but, the gearing being so low, this was a slow business and anyway the miller was not always in attendance.

When tail-winded the sails might turn against the brake and in the wrong direction when the brake is much less effective. If the wind were of sufficient force it might close the shutters of a patent-sailed mill by bending the fork-irons and with a gale on the back of a set of cloth-spread sails there was a real danger of the windshaft being tipped forward.

Southwold Great or Black Mill was considerably damaged in November 1863 being 'out of wind' and catching fire. It may have been as a consequence of this that it was rebuilt and modernised as described in chapter 2.

Other mills we know to have been tail-winded include Saxtead postmill (probably *c* 1853), Tuddenham St Mary smockmill in 1881, Chattisham smockmill in 1887, Knodishall postmill in 1908, Metfield towermill in 1916 and Walpole postmill in 1919. More recently Wenhaston mill, which had lost its fly some years previously, was caught out of wind and damaged in 1938 and then in March 1947 had its windshaft and sails torn right out in another gale. Also in that year Mr Jack Penton's postmill at Syleham was tail-winded as vividly described in *Windmills and Millwrighting* by Stanley Freese. During that storm Mr John Bryant of Pakenham mill was able to get the cap round just in time to avoid disaster.

Of course the power of the wind was not the only danger facing a windmill in a storm. Windmills generally being quite tall structures, and trees in the immediate vicinity being discouraged in order to allow free access to the wind from all directions, lightning strikes were by no mans an infrequent occurrence. Mr Clover of Drinkstone Mills recalled how he was flung from one side of his mill to the other when lightning struck and welded together the links of the sack-chain on its way to earth.

Other mills and millers were not so lucky. From *Rural Gleanings* by Orlando Whistlecraft, (published in 1851) we learn that a windmill at Blundeston was greatly damaged by lightning in June 1825 while one at Earl Stonham was 'shattered much' by the same agency in August 1837. He tells us of another, near Woodbridge, being struck in August 1843 and one of those at Gislingham suffering likewise in July 1848.

Other mills struck by lightning and badly damaged include Bungay towermill in 1918, Marlesford postmill *c* 1896, Ling's Mill, Mendlesham *c* 1914 and Thorndon postmill in 1923. Westhall postmill was struck the previous year when a Mr I. Beans, who was at the door of the roundhouse, was killed. Weston postmill was struck in 1896, caught fire and was destroyed and many other instances of mills being destroyed by fire may have emanated from lightning strikes.

However this was far from always being the case as fire could be caused by various means. In January 1784 the windmill near Claydon tollgate caught fire and 'was soon reduced to ashes'. It was reported a week later that the fire was occasioned by the 'friction of the gudgeon; hence we presume it necessary for every miller to examine those parts when he leaves off work'.[14] This postmill was rebuilt, worked until the 1890s and rather ironically was finally destroyed maliciously by fire in 1923.

A similar occurrence was responsible for the destruction of Rishangles composite mill on Sunday, the 21st February 1903. Mrs W. Last wrote in 1969[15] of the mill being overhauled and painted during the summer of 1902. Her father Mr R. Cuthbert, who was the miller, had said that afterwards some parts of the machinery got very hot when the wind was strong and the sails were going at speed. He had left the sails turning with the stones out of gear on the Saturday night: at about four o'clock on the Sunday morning his wife awoke to feed the baby and, as the window appeared 'bright', she looked out to see the mill on fire with the sails still turning. Mrs Last's brother cycled to Debenham to summon the fire brigade but the horses had to be got from a farm some distance away and by the time the brigade arrived the mill, stacked full of corn, was doomed.

The structure of a postmill, its contents and the presence of dust in the air made it extremely vulnerable to fire hazards. A report in the Suffolk Chronicle for 29 January 1859 concerns the postmill built in *c* 1806 close to the Cavalry barracks in Anglesea Road, Ipswich:

DESTRUCTION OF A WINDMILL BY FIRE—On Friday afternoon, shortly before three o'clock, a fire broke out in a mill on the Anglesea Road, the property of Miss Wright of St. Matthew's, and in the occupation of Mr. Nunn. Ignition from some unaccountable cause, commenced in the centre of the mill, and the man in charge was first made aware of its existence by observing flames issuing out of a small side window. An alarm was immediately given and the engine from the barracks (with a strong muster of soldiers, under the command of one of their officers) was quickly in attendance, as well as that from the Suffolk Fire Office and police station; but the mill being of wooden construction, all efforts to extinguish the flames were unavailing. In a short time the ponderous stones of which there were three pairs, fell with a tremendous crash, and by five o'clock a mere skeleton of the mill was left, although even then there was considerable fire in the roundhouse. There were about 100 sacks of corn, offal, etc. in the mill at the time, of which we were informed about 50 were saved, although considerably damaged by the water. The proprietor was insured, but not so the occupier, whose loss, unfortunately,

will be considerable, as in addition to the corn, etc., the internal fixtures were
his property.

What, one wonders, might these 'internal fixtures' be? A 'List of Tenants
Furniture' taken on 19 May 1831 in the postmill near Doe's Alley in Melton reads
as follows:

In the top story or Stage Floor
1 — Head strap
1 — Flour Mill right up Strap
1 — Do. Strap
2 — Jumper straps
1 — sack chain
1 — Do. Rope

In Stone Floor
1 — stone Rope
2 — stone Staves
2 — Levers
22 — Chill Bills
3 — Bill Thrifts
6 — Stone splines
2 — wrenches

In Grinding Floor
1 — Desk
1 — Gripe Line
2 — Leader Weights
1 — Flour Mill Rope
7 — Flour Bags
6 — Flour Cloths
2 — Brooms
2 — Brushes
1 — Bushel
3 — Sack carts
2 — Shovels

In the Loading Floor
1 — pair Scales
3 — Four Stone Weights
3 — Two Do.
1 — One Do.

1 — Four lb. Do.
1 — Two lb. Do.
1 — One lb. Do.
1 — Wire Sieve
1 — Nail Box
1 — Scraper
1 — Tin Skuttle
1 — Strike
1 — Sack Gigger
1 — Do. Rope
2 — Wheat Bags
3 — Sack Jacks
1 — Grind Stone[16]

Shortly after this the owner, John Wood, insured the mill with the Guardian Fire Assurance Co. for an annual premium of £2 2s 0d plus 12s duty. The mill, which had been built *c* 1800 was described as having a brick roundhouse and two pairs of stones and it was stated that there was 'no Kiln in the same nor adjoining thereto nor any Oats shelled theirin'. The sum insured was £400—'£200 on the Millwrights work and £200 on the stock in trade'.

Lightning strikes and bearing friction were not the only cause of mill fires. About 1915 Mr Fred Button's postmill at Mount Pleasant, Framlingham went up in flames after his boy who was smoking, dropped his lighted 'fag' when he heard Mr Button returning to the mill.

Other mills destroyed by fire included Badley 1833, Blaxhall 1883, Brandeston 1893, Gisleham 1911, Haughley by vandals 1940, Henley 1884, Nedging Tye 1909, Redgrave 1923, Rushmere St Andrew *c* 1939, Baggott's Mill Southwold 1876, Stoke Ash 1883, Battlesea Green Stradbroke 1898, Thornham Magna by vandals 1959, Wangford 1928, Whepstead 1894, Witnesham *c* 1908 and Wingfield *c* 1900. All the above were postmills with the exception of Redgrave, Rushmere and Wangford. Photographs of the latter mill as it burned were taken by a local resident.[17]

Apart from storm and fire, what other perils faced the old-time windmiller? Well, the earlier mills, particularly the low, cloth-sailed postmills, had their sails swinging dangerously close to the ground—'low enough to hit a pig' it has been said. The risk to the unwary of such a rapidly moving and nearly silent assailant resulted in many a fatality as happened to a servant of Mr Head, a baker in Bury St Edmunds, who going too near the sails of his master's mill was struck on the head and instantly killed.[18]

This fate also befell a Mr Bond at Sudbury,[19] Samuel Hood of Barton Mills,[20] John Porter at Bredfield[21] and the three year old son of Mr Walker, one-time miller at the two postmills on Stoke Hill, Ipswich.[22]

The grandfather of Mr G. A. Coles of Peasenhall shortened the sails of his postmill after they had struck the head of, and killed, a girl. Even with later, taller mills accidents with the sails occasionally occurred as with Mr James Dykes of Brandleston mill who was struck and killed as he stepped from the roundhouse loading door onto a load of corn on a cart. This was *c* 1888 and the late Mr Hart of Framsden remarked that Dykes had the sails painted red 'and they drew red out of him'.

Before the days of factory inspectors and safety regulations the unguarded gears and belt drives in wind and watermills provided yet another risk to the unwary or careless. Familiarity should never have bred contempt, for the gently whirring and clattering gears were an ever-present threat to anyone who strayed too close.

It is said that a miller named Bigsby was killed in Henley mill when his clothes caught in the gears. Years previously, in 1825 at Ling's postmill, Mendlesham the miller's nephew, William, a youth of thirteen was greasing some part for his uncle when his arm was drawn into the machinery and so severely injured that immediate amputation just above the elbow was necessary.[23]

With the introduction of engines for auxiliary power yet another source of potential danger was established. A single example will serve to illustrate this. In January 1890 at Wickham Skeith the miller, Mr Harry Roper, was working the towermill by means of the 8 hp steam engine as there was little wind. The boiler, which was said to have been overhauled only twelve months previously, burst causing damage estimated at £500. Mr Roper and two men, inside the mill, were unhurt but a boy, who was walking along a nearby path, was struck by falling bricks and gravely hurt.[24]

So the miller might lose limb or life or at least lose the source of his income although, after the insurance companies became established he need not be so financially distressed if he were prudent. At any rate it was a hard life, and although several old windmillers of my acquaintance have spoken with affection for their mills, others remembered them, and their work, as tough and exacting.

Suffolk windmills have not featured much in time of battle or war as have a few auspicious examples in other counties. In 1800 at the time of the threat of invasion by Napoleon and when food prices were particularly high, the poorer residents of Ipswich attacked Mr Savage's postmill on Stoke Hill, but were unable to force entry. Undeterred they swarmed into the tidemill near Stoke Bridge with cries of 'Bread, bread!' and were ejected only with difficulty by volunteer constables.[25]

A little later, in 1811, a company of soldiers on their way to Harwich to embark for the Peninsular War were able to assist with the erection of the postmill which stood in the village of Haughley until 1940.[5]

Although not suffering directly from enemy action several Suffolk windmills were demolished as a direct result of the two World Wars. The larger of the two towermills at Lavenham was almost completely dismantled during the first world war on the grounds that it afforded a mark for enemy aircraft. What target enemy planes might be seeking in the area is hard to imagine.

Walberswick marsh towermill suffered severe damage from gunnery practice during the last war whilst Kedington towermill was pulled down after being damaged by a crashing plane. The fine annular-sailed towermill at Haverhill was partially demolished early in the war, it was said, to facilitate low flying by aircraft from nearby airfields. It has been said that Parham postmill was finally pulled down for the same reason whilst Bramfield towermill was dismantled for the scrap iron it contained.

A perusal of local newspapers from the eighteenth century on shows a fair sprinkling of millers among bankrupts showing that although a number achieved a reasonable degree of affluence others, through bad management or just plain bad luck, failed to make a go of it. Thomas Winson of Rattlesden declaring his bankruptcy in 1890, stated that he had been in partnership with his brother many years previously but that the business had not been successful. He had then worked as a journeyman miller until 1887 when he recommenced business at Rattlesden. He complained that the mill he hired on lease at £24 p.a. was in such a bad state of repair that he had spent a considerable portion of his time in repairing it.[26] Eighty years previously Peter and William Sadler, millers at Little Waldingfield, for some inexplicable reason left the mill premises which they occupied as joint tenants. An advertisement in the Ipswich Journal for 30 June 1810 informed them that if they did not return and pay their rent between that date and 10 July a sale would be made of their remaining goods and chattels to defray the money owing.

The miller worked his mill, often dressed the stones and effected running repairs but the man who built the mills and carried out major overhauls and modernisations was the *millwright*. The old millwrights were the predecessors of today's mechanical engineers and, although originally concerned almost entirely with working in wood, latterly were equally dextrous with wrought and cast-iron. Their simple tools included the chisel and auger whilst heavy timbers would be cut to size over the sawpit and trimmed with an adze.

In 1782 Samuel Wright was a millwright with premises at Major's Corner, Ipswich and was still there, with his son, in 1844. In 1787 he advertised for six men who might have twelve months work at 'good country wages' if they were good hands. He added that 'none other need apply'.[27] In 1815 he built a smockmill on the site of the recently burnt postmill at Buxhall.

Nearby in Carr Street, Messrs Green and Browne were established as millwrights by 1811 but seem to have gone out of business before 1830, by which time one John Collins was operating from premises in Woodbridge Road.

Many small millwrighting concerns flourished throughout the county in the late eighteenth and nineteenth centuries. At Ballingdon, next to Sudbury, but then in Essex, Robert Hurwood was millwright in 1784, whereas William Hurwood (his son?) was declared bankrupt there in 1810. Ballingdon seems to have had more than its fair share of millwrights, there being no fewer than three listed in J. Pigot & Co.'s directory for 1830. By 1839 two of these had gone from the directory and Thomas Bear had appeared. We know of one windmill he built, at Lavenham in 1830–31, the building account for which is set out in appendix A.

He was followed before 1844 by William Bear, 'millwright and machine maker', who by 1855 had moved to premises, which included an iron and brass foundry, near the Market Hill. In 1860 Bear was responsible for building the large towermill at Buxhall on the foundations of the smock mentioned above. At this time one of Bear's most highly paid men was Robert Catchpole who was later to be acclaimed as the inventor of the air-brake which was given his name. The most interesting account for the building of Buxhall towermill is to be found in appendix C of *The English Windmill* by Rex Wailes. Another fine towermill, at Preston had certain similarities to Buxhall and probably was also built by Bear as may have been Stansfield towermill, dated 1840. Highfield smockmill on the Melford road out of Sudbury was similar in having a dome-shaped cap with gallery and, having been built in 1855 or soon after, was also likely to have been a product of Bear's firm.

Inscription in Drinkstone postmill

Inscribed post of Eye mill

By 1864 William Bear appears to have abandoned his millwrighting interests in Sudbury and from thenceforth was listed only as importer and manufacturer of millstones, still with premises at Sudbury until around 1875 and in Ipswich until a few years later. About 1863 or 1864 he moved his millwrighting business to Stowmarket, close to the railway station, but the venture does not seem to have been successful as his premises and stock in trade were up for auction in 1866.[28]

Robert Catchpole seems to have left Bear about then for a Robert Scase Catchpole, engineer and millwright, appears in the directories at Regent Street, Stowmarket from 1869 to 1904 and one wonders if he operated from his old master's late premises.

In East Suffolk the name Collins was long connected with the business of millwrighting. As well as the John Collins mentioned above in Ipswich a Jonathan Collins, who may well have been the same, was a millwright at Needham Market in 1825. There was also a William Collins, millwright in Framlingham. However by far the best know millwrighting firm to bear this name was that established in Melton in the late eighteenth century by Henry Collins. His works did not include a foundry and probably he obtained castings from the nearby Melton Ironworks.

The first mill which we know he tendered for and probably built was the slender black smock drainage mill which stood by the coastal road between Aldeburgh and Thorpeness. The original estimate dated 31 July 1800, and addressed To Mr Narnold of Aldeburgh, is preserved in the Moot Hall. It reads:

Timbered tower of oak principles to be built on the stud. 28 ft height by 17 ft diameter at the bottom. By twelve circle. With fantail $9\frac{1}{2}$ yards of cloth. Brake wheel 8 ft diameter, Main crosstry 23 inches Upright shaft 12. Pit wheel oak 9 ft diameter with clasp arms to shaft. For draining from 3 to 5 ft in length (Scoops). Grate to lanes or cuts. Large leaded cistern for cog wheel to work. To all head hooks, brakes, Grid irons and irons. Carting the mill or (?) board and lodgings of the men in the time of raising and completing the same for the sum of £470. 0. 0. Exclusive of cuts and drains in the Mead to the Mill and water lane for the scoops to work in and sluices if any wanted.

Delivered by me: Henry Collins,
Millwright of Melton.

From a photograph it is known that this mill had a small boat-shaped cap and the usual octagonal body. It is not clear from the above whether the *twelve circle* referred to the proposed diameter at the curb or the intention to make the mill twelve-sided.

In 1841–42 Collins are said to have moved four postmills from Melton or Woodbridge and it is probable that three of them were of those four which stood on Mill Hill Woodbridge as a postmill continued to work there until 1866. One was moved to Butley, another to Southwold (Bagott's) and a third to Ramsey, Essex where it still graces the village. The destination of the fourth is uncertain, but according to Jesse Wightman, was most likely to have been Ubbeston.

Three other windmills known to have been built by Collins were Pettaugh postmill on the site of an earlier mill in 1865, the smockmill which stood in Valley Road, Leiston and Chattisham smockmill probably in the same year as the millhouse which is dated 1867 although a mill is known to have stood there thirty years previously.

The firm, latterly Henry and Charles Collins, continued until about the turn of the century but it is unlikely that they built any new windmills after those mentioned above except possibly the windpump on Minsmere marshes described in Chapter 5. The declining years would have been spent in repair work and modernisation in a rather vain attempt to maintain the old wind and watermills in the face of increasing competition from the more modern roller installations.

The most famous millwrighting firm in Suffolk was that established by Nathaniel Whitmore in 1780 at Wickham Market. The premises, on the north side of the main street, included a foundry which eventually was enlarged in 1892 with three furnaces capable of melts of 5, 3 and 2 tons while bevel and spur gears up to 14 ft (4.27 m) in diameter could be moulded. When the founder died his son, John took over the business which flourished under his care. When he retired his sons carried on until, in 1868, the remaining son William N. took into partnership George Binyon, the firm changing its name to Whitmore and Binyon, although locally it was known as Wickham Ironworks. At this time the London offices and stores were moved from Gracechurch Street to Mark Lane, the firm also having an address in Ipswich.

The last change came in 1893 when William's son, W. J. Whitmore, was taken into partnership with his father. By this time the firm had extensive workshops including, not only the foundry, but a pattern shop, boiler shop, smithy, turnery, engine erecting shops and shops for the fitting up of roller-milling machinery. The drawing office was superintended by Mr A. Garrod. It was said that the most striking machine was one capable of turning and boring work-pieces up to a diameter of 20 ft (6.1 m).[29]   The entrance, flanked by iron pillars surmounted by spiked balls, and some of the office buildings at the front can still be seen but to appreciate how extensive were the works one should look at the illustration.

Whitmores are not known to have built any postmills from scratch although they were responsible for a large part of the rebuilding of Wetheringsett mill after it had been blown down in 1881. However in this instance the job was started by Samuel Clarke, a millwright from Debenham who ran into difficulties, so the owner called in Whitmore and Binyons to finish it.

It is probable that Whitmores were responsible for modernising many postmills during the first sixty or so years of the nineteenth century. This was particularly so with reference to the replacement of worn out wooden machinery with new equipment of cast iron. We know this to have been done at Framsden in 1836 and Saxtead in 1854, as mentioned in chapter 2, whilst at Saxtead they also fitted the Samson-head to the post. Judging by its close similarity with known examples, I am of the opinion that the tailstone installation in Ramsey mill is by Whitmores, and it is likely that other postmills outside Suffolk received their attention.

The similarity of the fan-carriage wheels and gearing on Framsden, Syleham, Thorpeness and Saxtead mills points to a common source, again presumably Whitmores, the arrangement on the latter mill having originally been fitted to Worlingworth Old Mill.

Whitmores are however better known for the fine and distinctive looking towermills which they built mainly in East Suffolk. A survey of these is included in chapter 3. The firm also put up tower mills further afield as at White Roding, Essex in 1877 and possibly Tendring and Milton Road Cambridge to judge from appearance. They even exported windmill machinery to be erected overseas; a mill of their manufacture is still standing in New Zealand, whilst another, now a house, is in Brisbane, Australia.

An advertisement of Whitmore and Binyon dated 1877 shows a smockmill and it is likely, from their appearance, that Cransford, Laxfield (built in 1842) and Westleton smockmills were their work.

Another product advertised in one of their catalogues was a small wind pump fitted with adjustable spring sails and largely of iron construction. One such example still stands just over the Norfolk border at Starston, but although several may have been erected in Suffolk no evidence has come to light to support this premise. From a number of newspaper advertisements it appears that Whitmores also acted as buying and selling agents for windmills.

Although in the earlier years Whitmores were concerned with the manufacture and erection of mills using stones and powered by wind, water and steam, in 1883 they commenced building roller mills both at home and abroad. These ranged from major installations in the large towns to miniature set-ups such as was to be seen in Reuben Rackham's mill just up the road in Wickham Market. The steam engine from this plant is now preserved at the Museum of East Anglian Life in Stowmarket.

Reuben's son, the late Edward Rackham, recounted how, as a child, he was held up by his father to meet Mr Binyon who was visiting his father's mill.

Whitmores were also sole agents for the plan-sifter and in their final years diversified their interests greatly, producing such equipment as rice mills and washers for ruby and diamond mines. When the Boer War broke out much of this demand ceased and this may have contributed to the once proud firm finally closing its doors in 1901.

Whitmore and Binyon's engineering works, Wickham Market

Many other references to millwrights exist, nearly all of them having been in business in quite a small way, as no doubt was John Scotchmer of Stowmarket in 1815 of whom a solitary mention occurs.

Of others, more recent, we know more. Robert Balls of Huntingfield, miller and millwright, and one Adams, an engineer from somewhere in the district, joined forces *c* 1864 to move a postmill buck from just over the Norfolk border to St James South Elmham where they erected it on a new trestle with round house.[30] A second postmill buck of unknown origin stood close by until recently.

Adams and Balls were also responsible for moving Cransford smockmill to its present site at Peasenhall *c* 1883.

Although this removal, like several others was accomplished without mishap the millwright's task, like the miller's was often fraught with danger. Raising a postmill in height was quite hazardous as was found at Debenham (see p. 42). Another instance occurred at Hartest in 1810 when a screw jack gave way allowing the mill to collapse. The millwrights engaged on this job were extremely fortunate; one who was on the second floor at the time, was discovered in the midst of the debris sitting across the post, quite unharmed. A second man, who had been operating one of the screw jacks, had the presence of mind to throw himself into an excavation in the ground and so avoided serious injury. An onlooker was not so lucky, however, and suffered a broken thigh.[31]

Robert Balls owned postmills at Walpole, Brundish and Metfield Common and had the top of an old buck at Whitehouse Farm Huntingfield which he used as a workshop.

Robert Martin, millwright of Beccles, built Blundeston towermill and in 1837 the finely proportioned towermill at Lound. He was succeeded by his son, Robert who was said to have built the brick windpump at Reydon Quay *c* 1890. Robert's son was followed by his son, also Robert, who should be noted as the inventor of a patent *smutter* (a machine for removing smut, a fungus, from the wheat), an example of which can be seen in Syleham mill. In turn *his* son, Neville Robert took over and although engaged in another branch of engineering, still finds time to do the occasional millwrighting job when required.

James Nunn was a millwright at Wenhaston in 1844 and is said to have helped build Westleton postmill a few years previously. Simon Nunn was working with his father in 1874 and carried on after his father's death. He is known to have worked on Saxtead mill and helped build the circular wooden roundhouse for Weston mill as well as fitting the fly from Pakefield to Wenhaston mill in 1881 or 1882. After the postmill at White House Farm, Huntingfield, built by his father only a few years previously, blew down in 1879 Si Nunn rebuilt it at a new site where it was worked by James Long before being taken over by Walter Aldridge. A little later Robert Martin fitted new sails to this mill and added a brick roundhouse.

Towards the end of the last century the millwright was being called on increasingly to demolish mills. Si Nunn bought the old postmill at Wenhaston Blackheath, which had been unused for several years, and pulled it down *c* 1896.

Mention has been made of postmill bucks being moved to new sites and it happened that quite often they were not re-erected as postmills but simply allowed to stand on the ground perhaps elevated on bricks to discourage rot. Looking like tall, rather elegant sheds they could be used for a variety of purposes.

When Badwell Ash mill was demolished *c* 1930 parts were used to build a tall oil engine powered mill, having the appearance of a postmill buck but not retaining the original framing. This still stands, as does a true buck now furnished with a tiled roof at Creeting St Mary. This has been in its present position for many years and at one time was used as a nesting house for pigeons. It is not on a mill site but was probably moved from a known site in the parish, on higher ground about half a mile away.

A buck from Cross Street, Hoxne was moved $4\frac{1}{2}$ miles (7.25 km) to Worlingworth and set up as a steam mill. It was finally taken down *c* 1910. Another buck, which was placed on the ground after the mill was taken down, was that of Mansfield's mill at Hundon. When Little Glemham mill was demolished the buck was carried to Theberton where it was used as a steam mill driving one pair of stones. In this case the removal entailed a journey of around nine miles (14.5 km) the body presumably being carried whole on a timber 'drug', hauled by a traction engine, although prior to the introduction of these, about 1860, power would have been provided by a team of horses or oxen. Another buck moved by traction engine was taken from Magpie Green, Wortham to Walsham-le-Willows where it stood alongside the postmill and served as a steam mill with stones belt-driven by a Ruston and Hornsby $9\frac{1}{2}$ hp engine in a nearby shed.

A tiny postmill buck, this time from the Aldeburgh or Orford area where it is reputed to have been a drainage mill, was moved to Saxtead where it stood for many years in the same yard as the present mill until being moved to Jesse Wightman's father's garden opposite where it was still to be seen in 1938.

Finally, when Aldridge's mill, Huntingfield was pulled down in 1928 the top of the buck was moved to Westhall Common where it kept the postmill there company for several years.

Returning to millwrights, we come to Ted Friend, who was born around 1876 and apprenticed to Si Nunn. He spent some of his working life at Whitmore and Binyons and later settled in Aldeburgh. Friend worked on many windmills in the area, one of his early jobs being to help Si Nunn build the wooden roundhouse for Weston mill. Nunn sent Friend to cut out the roundhouse curb on a saw bench at Darsham mill after which he built it up at Weston and effected various repairs to sails and machinery. Finishing late one night Friend, a little fellow, had to carry his tools all the way home to Wenhaston on foot—a distance of seven miles. (11.25 km). Friend also worked, with Nunn, on the Walberswick marshmill.

Later Ted Friend was employed as carpenter and millwright for the Thorpeness Estate and during this time, in the winter of 1922–3, supervised the removal of Aldringham postmill to Thorpeness where it was modified to pump water into the nearby 'House in the Clouds' water tower. A detailed account of this event is to be found in *Windmills and Millwrighting* by Stanley Freese.

An illustration of the millwrights' prowess is related to this mill. During the last war, while the mill was still winding itself some children blocked the tramway causing the steps and fly to lift several feet and the buck to tilt forward. The Estate foreman, Mr Staff, called in a friend of his, an army Sergeant Major who mobilised some of the locally stationed militia to help.

A number of men sat on the steps and fly frame but to no avail. Ted Friend was called and looking over the mill quickly sized up the situation. With a sledge hammer tap here and there he soon had the mill level again where brute force had failed completely!

Aldringham mill removal was one of the last to be accomplished but in the eighteenth and nineteenth centuries such an event was by no means uncommon. Postmills were always considered to be portable although of course, if the mill were to have a brick roundhouse, this would be built from scratch after the trestle and buck were erected on their new site.

The open-trestle postmill which perched on Eye Castle mound, and is mentioned in chapter 2, was transported to Cranley Green *c* 1845 and was later heightened, modernised and furnished with a tall roundhouse.

Alpheton postmill was said to have been moved from Shimpling *c* 1875 by two teams of horses whilst it was also rumoured that the postmill which used to stand on Barking Tye came from a site in the south of Gosbeck parish early last century. However this seems dubious as a mill is shown on Hodskinson's 1783 map on Barking Tye but nothing is shown on any known map at the alleged Gosbeck site.

Bedingfield postmill, of which the tarred roundhouse alone remains, came from Oakley on a timber drug in 1828 and a large postmill in Kings Road, Bury St Edmunds, was a few years after this conveyed to Wickhambrook where it was later worked by William Fuller. Darsham postmill was moved from another location in the village early in the last century and a postmill from Felsham was transported by a team of horses to Gedding in 1867 and set up next to an old open-trestle mill. Fornham St Martin open-trestle mill was also reputed to have been moved but it is not known where it went.

From Mount Pleasant, Framlingham *c* 1855 a postmill went to Tannington where it was finally blown down on 10 August 1879. A postmill at Hadleigh was moved to Elmsett to become Ladbrook's mill.

It has been said that Honington postmill was brought from Sapiston in 1853 but there seems to be some doubt about this from the evidence of available maps. One of the Hopton postmills came from Bardwell in 1834.[32]

Several postmills which stood in Ipswich are said to have been moved from the borough as in 1849 when one of the mills on Stoke Hill had to be taken down as a result of the building of the tunnel for the Eastern Union Railway line from Colchester to Ipswich. This mill was re-erected at Earl Soham where it stood until 1903 or 1904. It was an old-style mill with mortised wooden windshaft and cloth sails but when the windshaft broke *c* 1880 Whitmore and Binyon furnished it with an iron shaft and Patents. The postmill which stood on Bishop's Hill is also believed to have been removed in 1866 to Offton where it was put up alongside another postmill moved from Elmsett.

The buck of Leavenheath mill is said to have come from Middleton, just over the Essex boundary near Sudbury, whilst Letheringham postmill reputedly went to Charsfield.

Other postmill removals include Kersey's mill, Mendlesham, said to have come from Otley *c* 1840, Thurston from Pakenham in 1750 to replace an earlier mill, a tiny mill at Bower House Tye, Polstead possibly from Stoke by Nayland *c* 1880 and Syleham from Wingfield *c* 1823.

A postmill at Thelnetham was moved to Diss in Norfolk in 1818 while in the same year a mill of unknown type, called 'Lower Mill', at Stanton was *removed whole* but where to we are not told.

Worlingworth New Mill was brought from Ufford in 1848 and it was rumoured that Chippenhall Green mill, Fressingfield stood until 1792 at one of the South Elmhams although a mill is shown at the later site by Hodskinson. Badingham 'New Mill' was moved from a nearby site near Colston Hall by Whitmore and Binyons *c* 1870.

Several smockmill removals have been recorded, Gt Thurlow having been brought from Slough, Bucks in 1807 and a smockmill in Tuddenham Road, Ipswich having been transported to Kettleburgh probably *c* 1855, where it was worked in conjunction with a watermill. Westerfield smockmill was moved a short distance and re-erected *c* 1820.

Probably the most travelled smockmill in the county was the very small one-pair mill which stood at Saxtead Lodge Farm, Framlingham until 1921. This had started life as a marshmill somewhere and was then moved to the farm opposite Ufford 'Crown' and converted to corn grinding. From thence it was moved to Hacheston by Whitmore and Binyon and set up at Bridge Farm. As if this were not enough it was shortly moved again, bodily with sails on, across a couple of fields to a neighbouring farm but ere long it travelled to its final resting place *c* 1890 where it was worked for the farm until around the outbreak of the first World War.

To return once more to millwrights it should be remarked that just as Suffolk millwrights sometimes built mills outside their county, so millwrights from elsewhere built here. Hunts of Soham are a case in point having put up Gt Bradley towermill in 1839 and Little Thurlow smock in 1865.

Of Suffolk millwrights it remains to mention but a few more. William Page of Needham Market, who was in business from about 1860 until early this century, built Gosbeck postmill on the site of an earlier mill between 1865 and 1868.

Cockfield towermill was built in 1891 by Brewer and Sillitoe of Long Melford to replace a tiny towermill on the same site called Pepper Mill. Henry Brewer was stated to be a mechanical engineer in the 1869 directory while as late as 1929 a C. Sillitoe was still listed as millwright at Melford. Sillitoe worked on Swilland mill and was also responsible for fitting the cast iron canister to the wooden windshaft for Mr Clover's father at Drinkstone postmill. As originally fitted it worked loose and he had to add the large iron split clamp which has sufficed to hold the assembly rigid. Another millwright operating in 1869 was William Brook of Palgrave who was followed by Robert and finally by Henry Brook who was still doing repair work in the 1920s.

Sam Clarke of Debenham has already been mentioned in connection with Wetheringsett mill. His father, also Samuel, was apprenticed to William Collins of Framlingham before becoming a millwright based at Weybread. Old Sam had two other sons, one of whom, William who worked for Whitmore and Binyon, gained the strange nickname 'Truthy'. It was he who pulled down the fine

Amos Clarke, millwright at Pakenham mill in 1950

Jesse Wightman, millwright in 1938

postmill at Saxmundham in 1907. Young Sam had three sons, two of whom Amos and George, followed their father's and grandfather's calling. George lived at Debenham while Amos, who was originally a wheelwright, settled in Ipswich. Amos did most of the work re-erecting Aldringham mill at Thorpeness and was also instrumental in the restoration work carried out on Stanton postmill between 1938 and 1941. However by the time he was practising his craft, there was much more call for demolition than building of mills, for he told Stanley Freese, on the occasion of his dismantling Earl Soham postmill in 1947, that it was the 79th he had wholly or partially taken down. He said that he did not pull over mills bodily, except during the 1914–18 war under Government orders, because he would rather salvage as much of the materials as possible for his own use. He also voiced the opinion that the Sussex practice of pulling over postmills with traction engines was proof of a lack of understanding of postmill construction because a sound mill could not be dislodged in this manner without first cutting a main timber, and if the right timber were cut the traction engine would not be necessary!

Other mills we know Amos Clarke to have demolished during a long career were Botesdale Smock soon after 1918, Chediston, Wickham Skeith and Hasketon towermills, in 1925, Ipswich Lattice Lane smock *c* 1930, Grundisburgh postmill *c* 1930, Shadingfield smock in 1938/9 and the trestle of the second Earl Soham postmill also in 1947.

In 1920 Amos carried out some repairs on Chillesford Lodge drainage mill but after being marooned there by floods, declared he would have no more to do with marshmills!

Amos's sons Alfred and George also did some millwrighting: Alfred was reputedly a fine craftsman and helped his father on the Thorpeness rebuild; George assisted on the dismantling of the Earl Soham mills.

By 1933 the only millwright mentioned in Kelly's directory was Frank Blake of Dallinghoo; strangely enough this was also the first time he was entered, although he was 58 years of age at the time.

The other twentieth century millwright, who operated mostly in the eastern half of Suffolk, is Jesse E. Wightman who was born at Brandeston, resided for many years at Saxtead and now lives in Essex. Mr Wightman worked on many windmills between the two wars and is a veritable mine of information, remembering not only details of their interior economy but dates relating to them going back long before his time and almost invariably accurate to the day. He assisted Mr Aldred, miller at Saxtead, with maintaining the mill from 1926 and later was responsible for much of the work carried out to restore the mill which will be described in a later chapter.

From the foregoing it will be seen that the typical millwright was a fearless man, well versed in the intricacies of his trade as well he should be, usually having been apprenticed for seven years—and nearly always a bit of an individualist if not a real 'character'. Usually he was successful at his job but occasionally things went wrong as at Shotley towermill *c* 1880 when new sails were being fitted. These were put up but not properly secured when the men went for a drink at Shotley 'Boot'. A sudden gust of wind caught the sails, breaking them off and the mill never worked by wind again.[33]

Another specialist, who sometimes combined his trade with that of millwrighting, was the millstone manufacturer. He would obtain Peak stones from quarries in Derbyshire and Yorkshire and import Burrs from France to make up into finished stones. French stones were always an expensive item, an average price in Ipswich between 1320 and 1347 being £1 16 11. 7/10d presumably for a pair.[2] In the 1860s William Bear was quoting £29 for a pair of 4 ft 6 ins (1.37 m) French stones, which seems very reasonable as a contemporary reference book quotes £60 the pair and £27 for a similar sized pair of Peak stones.[34]

William Tinsley was established as a millstone builder at Bridge Wharf, Stoke, Ipswich in 1866 but may have died fairly soon after as Mrs Ann Tinsley had taken over by 1879. From *c* 1885 for about ten years the firm continued under the name of W. Tinsley & Co., in Commercial Road, opposite the old Great Eastern Railway goods station. A 4 ft (1.22 m) Burr runner stone bearing Tinsley's nameplate can be seen in Framsden mill and was last used by Mr E. S. Webster for grist *c* 1936. This stone came from Otley smockmill when that was demolished *c* 1908.

Whitmore and Binyon also built millstones and the only other manufacturer listed was William Irving of Gt Whip Street, Ipswich, in 1875. In 1874 George King of Princes Street, Ipswich and Webb and Sons of Combs were listed as millband manufacturers and Jonathan Wood of Whitton was noted as a mill bill manufacturer as were Charles Cunnell of Wickham Market and Daniel Day of Whip Street, Ipswich in 1891.

Stone-dressers were sometimes itinerant tradesmen and as such do not figure in old directories. In fact they appear in retrospect as shadowy figures, for references to them are slight. The satisfactory dressing of millstones, particularly French stones for flour grinding, was however a skilled job which normally took years to master. Many windmillers and watermillers learnt this trade and dressed their own stones whilst millwrights also often combined this skill with those more directly concerned with their trade. Jesse Wightman gained the reputation of being a good stone-dresser but today only a handful of men in the whole country can claim to be masters of this craft.

Inscribed sidegirt in Framsden postmill

Inscribed brick in Tricker's mill, Woodbridge

5

Marshmills and Pumps

The marsh drainage windmills of Suffolk were nowhere near as numerous as their Norfolk neighbours and, almost without exception, were concentrated in three relatively small areas. These were on the Suffolk side of the Lark and Little Ouse Rivers on the north-west boundary, on the River Waveney to the north-east and on the eastern coastal marshes.

Very little regarding the history of these mills has been documented but it seems probable that those bordering the Cambridgeshire Fens were the first to be built. The earliest wind powered engines for fen drainage were constructed around 1580 and it is probable that these were of wooden construction but fixed (i.e. not able to turn to wind) as pictured in *The English Improver Improved*, by Walter Blith, published in 1652.

The north-west corner of the county falls within that fen area known as the Bedford Level. For some time before the seventeenth century the frequent flooding of this area had caused concern and piecemeal attempts at drainage had been attempted. In 1630 the Earl of Bedford undertook to drain this area of the southern fens which later was to take his family's name and to this end he employed the Dutch engineer, Cornelius Vermuyden, who was experienced in this type of work having undertaken projects in Yorkshire as well as in his native country.

Although much was achieved, a judgement of 1638 declared the Earl's undertaking to be defective and in the same year the king (Charles I) undertook to finish the job, retaining the services of Vermuyden. During the Civil War (1642–9) the project was abandoned and some of those people who objected to the work of the drainers, took advantage of the situation, and destroyed much of what had been achieved, whilst other of the works were neglected and allowed to deteriorate.

Immediately after the war an act of parliament decreed that the then Earl of Bedford, who had succeeded his father in 1641, should undertake the completion of the draining of the Great Level by 1656.

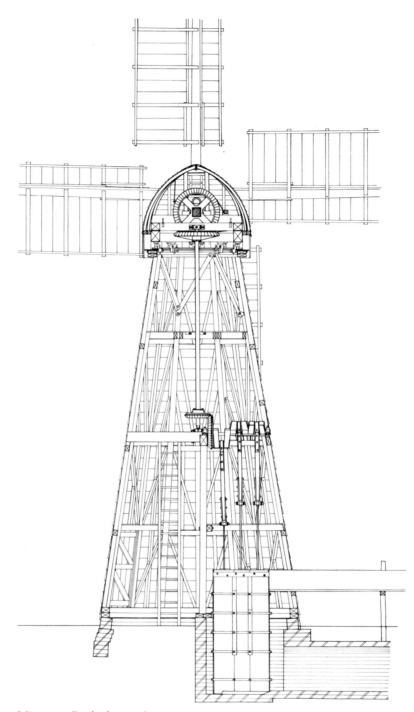

Minsmere, Eastbridge windpump

It should be noted that earlier undertakings had merely aimed at removing the water from the land during the summer months and that winter floods might still inundate these summer pastures. The aim of this second stage of drainage was to provide pasture and arable land throughout the whole year.

Against great difficulties, including a lack of money as well as the antipathy of a number of fenlanders, the great work progressed, until in 1652 it was adjudged to be completed.

I have leaned heavily on Dr H. C. Darby's admirable treatise, *The Draining of the Fens*[1] for much of this introductory material. It appears that subsequent to the draining, briefly described above, serious problems arose due to silting-up of the river outfalls and shrinkage of the drained fenland peat resulting in a gradual lowering of the level of the land.

By 1700 much of what had been achieved and acclaimed was in ruins and inundations were once again commonplace. To the end of improving the situation increasing numbers of wind engines were erected near the dykes and drains to lift flood water, which flowed down from the surrounding higher land, and discharge it into the waterways that it might find its way to the sea.

Walter Blith described three types of mechanism which might be wind powered and employed for lifting water for the purpose of draining. These were the scoop wheel, the chain and bucket pump and the screw. The windpumps of the time may still have been of the type illustrated by Blith but it is probable that a number were of the smock type, with tailpole for winding, as introduced from Holland by Vermuyden.

Although the mills provided the only means of clearing the flood water they were often condemned as they interfered with the watercourses by introducing mud into them and, being put up piecemeal by landowners, would drain one area at the expense of a neighbouring locality.

Despite these problems in 1727 an Act was passed which in principle meant that drainage by mills was accepted thereby creating a precedent which was to be widely followed. This meant that responsibility for local drainage schemes within the main system was vested in local landowners. Mills were erected to lift water from the main drains into the rivers and if necessary two mills were 'ganged' so as to share the lift if one proved insufficient to cater with the head of water.

It is not known how many of these mills were erected on the Suffolk side of the River Lark but Hodskinson shows six on his map of 1783, one of which was located just north of the present county boundary, in Cambridgeshire. On the west bank in Cambridgeshire stood another three. Of those in Suffolk one stood away from the river bank on the side of a drain, presumably assisting its neighbour in achieving the necessary lift. The area was at that time denoted as Mildenhall Fen to the north, Mildenhall Mow Fen in the centre and Mildenhall Common Fen towards the south, all three being bounded by the Mildenhall

Drove and Drain on the east beyond which lay Lakenheath Town Moor and Mildenhall Common.

Although these measures did something to alleviate conditions the situation was still far from satisfactory early in the nineteenth century.

R. G. Baker, on a map published in 1821[2] indicates five Suffolk mills apparently in the same positions as those shown on the one-inch Ordnance Survey of the area, published in 1836. Greenwood marks only two of these River Lark mills in 1824 but Bryant, two years later, was more thorough showing five although the positions of two do not appear to agree with those on the OS map. One of these, standing by an embankment known as Cross Bank, was indicated by Bryant and Greenwood and had presumably disappeared before 1836 whereas by then a new mill had been erected a little more than four miles up river near West Row.

Two mills, close together on White Top Mill Drain were named on the OS as 'White Top Mills' while another, further south was called 'Middle Mill'.

One of the White Top Mills was said to have been of smock type with scoop-wheel[3] whilst the sole survivor, Middle Mill, is also of the smock type, its low octagonal brick base although only about 8 ft (2.44 m) high being broad at about 24 ft (7.3 m) across faces (outside). Above this a portion of smocking about a further 11 ft (3.45 m) high is topped with a pyramidal tiled roof, the conversion into a dwelling having been recently completed.

It appears that by the 1840s the area was judged to be satisfactorily drained. William White in his History, Gazetteer and Directory of Suffolk, published in 1844, stated that the western corner of the county, consisting of about 15000 acres (6000 hectares) of *low fen*, was then well drained and cultivated. He remarked that in Mildenhall parish the fen land was divided into two districts, one of which, containing about 3000 acres (1200 hectares), was called Burnt Fen First District[4] and consisted of those lands which were allotted to the 'adventurers' who executed the drainage act during the reign of Charles II. The other portion was called Mildenhall Fen or Burnt Fen Second District and comprised 5640 acres (2280 hectares), allotted to the owners of the adjacent lands. The windpumps could not take all credit for the excellent state of affairs as by then two pumps powered by steam engines had been installed.

Arthur Young, the famous agriculturalist who was born at, and lived in, Bradfield Combust near Bury St Edmunds published his *General View of the Agriculture of the County of Suffolk* in 1794.[5] He remarked that there were few instances of such great and sudden improvements as were made during the eighteenth century in the Burnt Fen of Lackford Hundred which comprised more than 14000 acres (5670 hectares). Forty years previously 500 acres (200 hectares) of it were let for a guinea a year but in 1772 an act was obtained for a separate drainage and 1s 6d an acre levied for the expense of embankments, *pumping mills* and other requisites. Of course, at this date, the pumping mills were wind-powered as it was not until 1817–18 that the first steam engine was put to work in the fens.[6] In 1777 the bank broke and most of the proprietors were ruined but within five years the drainage was so much improved that it 'occasioned some persons to purchase in this neglected tract. The banks were better made, mills erected, and the success was great.'[7]

On the edge of the fenland, in Lakenheath parish stood a few more wind pumps, one close by the bank of a drain known as Lakenheath New Load (*sic* = Lode) being named Turf-fen Mill on the 1836 OS map. This mill was also noted by Greenwood and Bryant and is believed to have been of the smock type.

Another smockmill at the junction of the Little Ouse River and Twelve Foot Drain stood, in ruinous condition, until *c* 1949. This was near an earlier site marked by Hodskinson as well as Greenwood and Bryant who named it 'Crosswaters Mill'. From a photograph it is known to have had a boat shaped cap and what look like common sails. Winded by means of a braced tailpole and driving the usual scoop wheel it was known as 'Old Lode Mill' and 'Great Fen Mill' and may have been moved from the earlier location. Greenwood alone showed a second mill close by on the northern bank of the Little Ouse but presumably it went soon after his survey as nothing more is known of it.

At the time of Hodskinson's survey a substantial area north of Prickwillow and bounded by the Ouse and Little Ouse rivers was included in Suffolk but this was shortly afterwards transferred to Cambridgeshire (Isle of Ely) and is not included in this survey.

The second district to be considered is the marshland on the Suffolk side of the River Waveney. Drainage mills were scattered over this wide area from Barsham Marshes, west of Beccles all the way down to Cobholm Island on the south bank of Breydon Water.

Although Hodskinson's map shows several of these mills it seems probable that most were built during the first half of the nineteenth century as were the majority of their Broadland Norfolk neighbours. That piecemeal attempts at drainage had been made earlier is witnessed by Gillingwater, who wrote that prior to 1652 a breakwater was formed on the sandy isthmus, between Lowestoft and Kirkley, to prevent the sea from inundating the surrounding marshes whenever a violent storm arose from the north-west in conjunction with a spring tide.[8] At a commission of sewers, held at Lowestoft in February 1660, an order was made that Cornelius Vermuyden or some other engineer at London should be requested to visit the town to advise on the embankments to be erected there following a breach by the sea. It was further ordered that a levy be sent to the several towns chargeable to the sea-breach at Lowestoft, at double the proportion which was formally charged viz: 'from the said sea-breach to Beccles Bridge and Gillingham Dam, in the whole level, chargeable at two shillings in the pound;

and from the said Bridge and Dam to Ditchingham Dam and Bungay Bridge at sixteen pence in the pound'.[9]

Despite these works, and subsequent strengthenings of the defences, the sea broke through in 1717 but repairs were effected and Defoe, travelling through Norfolk, a few years later, stated that 'above 40,000 Scots cattle were brought down to feed in this country each year, the majority of them in the rich pastures between Norwich, Beccles and Gt Yarmouth.'[10]

It is probable that some of the earlier mills in this district were of smock type but of those which survived later most, again like their Norfolk counterparts, were towermills. A plan, dated 1849 of Worlingham Hall Estate shows the mill just east of Worlingham Staithe behind the river wall. An undated engraving[11] pictures it as a small towermill with anti-clockwise common sails apparently in a wooden poll-end, a steep boat-cap and braced tail-pole.

A mile (1.6 km) eastwards along the river bank, in the parish of North Cove, stood another towermill of yellow brick with the usual boat-shaped cap, common to the district. By 1934 the cap was off exposing the iron windshaft and brakewheel. After the mill went out of use many years previously a portable steam engine was used for a while before an oil engine was installed driving a turbine pump.

Other mills on this stretch of marshland included Black Mill and Castle Mill, (the latter with turbine pump) in North Cove parish, Hober Mill in Barnby parish and Share Mill in the parish of Carlton Colville. Several of these mills were converted to work by steam in a river development scheme of 1884. On Oulton Marsh were Skepper's mill and Arnold's mill, the base of whose tower still stands. This mill may have had a scoop wheel at one time but latterly was motor driven with a vertical turbine pump; it carried common sails and was tailpole winded.

On Blundeston Marshes another drainage mill stood which had gone out of use by wind before the turn of the century.

A mile and a half (2.4 km) further downstream stood another, very small towermill on Somerleyton Marshes. This has been a roofed-over stump for many years while, in an adjacent shed, there used to be a horizontal single-flue Britannia boiler and steam engine using coal stored in the mill base.

Next we come to that gem of marshmills, this time a smockmill, at Herringfleet. This little black, tarred cloth-sailer, the last of its type, is in the care of the County Council and of late has been run, wind permitting, on several occasions each year.

Although not shown on the Inclosure Award map of 1819 Bryant shows a mill here and it is thought to have been built by Robert Barnes, a Yarmouth millwright, about 1820. A map of 1883 shows the mill as disused but some time after then its owners, the Somerleyton Estate Trustees, put it back to work and maintained it and doubtless this has allowed it to survive.

The mill is winded by a braced tailpole carrying a geared hand-winch at its lower end, a chain from the winch drum being hitched to successive wooden posts in the ground surrounding the mill. The boat shaped cap turns on a 'dead' curb with wooden blocks in place of the customary rollers while there are but two centering wheels and no keep flange.

The mill contains three floors and on the ground floor is a couch and fireplace without flue which meant that the smoke had to find its way up and out of the mill. These refinements were for the comfort of the marshman who would spend all night in the mill if the weather demanded his continuing attention. The marshman was also responsible for clearing the dykes; the last marshman Charlie Howlett served the mill for many years from 1923, before which the marshman was Jimmy Walker and the mill was known locally as Walker's mill.

Herringfleet mill has anti-clockwise sails carried on an iron windshaft 6 ins (152 mm) diameter while the smallish wooden brakewheel with fifty-nine teeth meshes with a forty-seven tooth mortise-wheel wallower which is really a spur wheel 4 ft 6 ins (1.37 m) diameter. The $11\frac{3}{4}$ ins (300 mm) square wooden upright shaft carries at its lower end a thirty-three tooth iron bevel wheel engaging with the large iron *pit-wheel* with 102 wooden cogs. This is carried on an 8 in (203 mm) diameter shaft on which is cast 'W. T. ENGLAND MILLWRIGHT YARMOUTH 1910'.

The 'scoop-wheel', outside the mill tower, is 16 ft (4.88 m) diameter and is of iron with thirty wooden paddles which taper from 13 ins (330 mm) to 9 ins (228 mm) wide at the tips. It runs in a closely fitting culvert and is covered with a boarded hoodway. It can be seen, that with an overall ration of 1:2.46 the scoop-wheel will turn at 6 rpm when the sails are going at 15 rpm which they do when spinning in a stiff breeze. From the foregoing it seems likely that the mill would pump at the rate of perhaps 2000 gpm (9000 litres/min) in favourable conditions. The wooden brake has a long lever, or *fang-staff*, projecting through the rear gable and carrying two chains for pulling the brake on and off. Herringfleet mill worked until the scoop-wheel was damaged in 1955. In latter days an oil engine provided assistance but the mill proved adequate until Yarmouth Bar was deepened and the tidal surge of the river increased. After going out of use an electric pump was installed.

Now in Fritton parish, near the ruins of St Olave's Priory, stands a quaint little structure which we will call a 'trestle mill' as the 4 cant-posts stand on short cross-trees with twin iron rod 'quarter-bars', the whole resting on a low concrete base. This tiny mill was built in 1910 or 1912 by W. T. England on the site of a smock drainage mill, very similar to Herringfleet mill, removed in 1898. This mill had been derelict for some years and the surrounding marshes were then drained by sluices until the great flood of 1910. It was then thought by local inhabitants, who objected to the smell of the water lying on the marshes, that a windpump would drain better.

So it was around this time that the mill was built for Lord Somerleyton to drain about 100 acres (40 hectares) and worked in conjunction with Priory Farm. It was variously known as 'Pony Mill', 'Butterfly Mill' and 'Mallett's Mill', after the name of the tenant farmer at Priory Farm when the mill was built.

Winded by an eight-bladed fly and carrying patent sails of only six bays with external Y-wheel and control chain the mill was painted white and maintained in perfect condition. Iron gearing drove the small scoop-wheel which was only about 3 ins (76 mm) wide and access to the fly and miniature cap was by an external ladder at the tail.

The sail-shutters and fan-blades were replaced on several occasions by Englands, one such occurrence being commemorated in pencil on one of the cant-posts with the date, August 20th 1923.

In 1953 the mill was struck by lightning, one stock being split and two sails blown off. These were reinstated but by 1957 the little mill had become virtually redundant owing to the ever increasing intensity of tides on the River Waveney which necessitated the installation of an electric pump nearby.[12]

Next along the river bank, about half a mile west from St Olave's mill, stands the derelict tower of Fritton Marsh mill. First shown on the 1837 OS map, this typical small mill with patent sails, boat-shaped cap and six-bladed fly was still in perfect order before the last war. The tarred, red-brick tower measures 10 ft (3.05 m) diameter at ground level where the brickwork is 18 ins (457 mm) thick and tapers to 8 ft (2.44 m) diameter at the curb which carries an upturned iron rack. There were never any proper windows in the tower, only wooden traps which have since disappeared.

The broad sails with canvas covered iron-framed shutters were controlled by an external chain passing over a Y-wheel and held away from the tower by a braced wooden guide in typical 'Norfolk' fashion.

The iron brakewheel with fifty-eight wooden cogs carried an iron brake band with thirty-five separate wooden blocks screwed to it. The thirty-two tooth iron wallower is mounted on a square wooden upright shaft while the pit-wheel was of all wooden construction and measured 7 ft 4 ins (2.24 m) diameter with about eighty cogs. The scoop-wheel was only 5 ins (127 mm) wide and 11 ft (3.36 m) diameter and was housed in the usual horizontally boarded hoodway or 'paddle-pox'.

Inside the mill the following inscriptions occur. 'R. E. MARTIN JUNE 6th 1895; S. HIGH; C. MARTIN.' The last marshman who worked the mill was Alban Pettingell, who took over the job from his father Ted, and worked on the level for some fifty years. The mill was said to have worked almost without a hitch apart from the fact that the constant surge of the Waveney tide, together with the wash created by the revolving scoop-wheel, gradually destroyed the wooden baulks upon which the mill was built.

In 1946 the brickwork at the base of the mill started crumbling as the baulks had

Fritton Warren trestle mill in 1937

Fritton tower marshmill in 1937

rotted and in 1948 the bricks finally gave way and smashed the scoop-wheel. Shortly after this Pettingell and one of his brothers removed the sails and fly, but presumably repaired the scoop-wheel as a drive from a tractor to the pit-wheel was arranged and continued to work until *c* 1961. About this time an electric pump was installed by Smithdale and Sons of Acle.

Further north in Fritton parish, near Fritton Warren stood another small trestle mill, similar to that near St Olave's Bridge and put up by W. T. England in, it is thought, 1910.

This little mill differed from St Olave's mill in several ways. Here the 'quarter-bars' or cant-post braces were of wood, 4 ins (102 mm) wide and 7 ins (178 mm) deep and were much more prominent extending about halfway up the tower and splaying out to the ends of the 10 ins (254 mm) by $4\frac{1}{2}$ ins (114 mm) 'cross-trees'. Two of the quarter-bars were exposed and two boarded over to connect with the tower thus giving the mill a curious pyramidal silhouette at the bottom.

Patent sails about 5 ft (1.52 m) wide were controlled with an external striking chain as at St Olave's but the more usual six-bladed fly was in evidence whilst the external access ladder was of iron instead of wood. Also, unlike St Olave's mill, this one drove a turbine pump with a side-hinged sluice gate.

By 1937 the cap had gone (if a cap as such there had been) but the mill was still serviceable. The mill had all iron gearing, the upright shaft being very slender and the brakewheel and wallower very small whilst the iron brake band closed on a flange on the front face of the brake-wheel. Apparently this odd little structure was pulled down *c* 1948 and nothing remains now.

Before we leave Fritton, travelling downstream towards Breydon Water, we come to the tower of another drainage mill of tarred red brick with scoop-wheel and the usual boat-shaped cap. This is all that remains of another fine little mill which was in perfect repair before the last war.

A mill is shown on or near this site on maps back to Hodskinson but the earliest date in the mill is 1844. Known as Bell Hill Mill from the nearby tumulus of that name and also as Caldecott Mill it was purchased from the Somerleyton Estate with Caldecott Hall *c* 1925 by a Mr Dashwood. It was last worked by Mr Ben Hewitt who followed his father.

It carried the usual broad Norfolk-style patent sails with shutters 4 ft 10 ins (1.47 m) and 3 ft 10 ins (1.17 m) wide, sweeping close to the ground. An iron-railed gallery was furnished to the cap and the external striking-chain was carried on a braced guide pole. A prominent eight-bladed fly was carried high up and close in to the cap. The scoop-wheel 15 ft 9 ins (4.8 m) diameter is carried on a square wooden shaft.

Around 1937, due to the tower beginning to lean, two iron bands were fitted by Mr J. K. Thrower and at the same time a new pitch-pine stock was fitted and the pit-wheel re-cogged. However by 1940 the mill was considered unsafe and an electric pump was installed. A few years later the sails and fly were taken down, and one stock and two sails found a new home in Pettingell's Mill on the Norfolk side of the river. When Mr Francis Brooks took over from Hewitt in 1948 he removed most of the cogs from the pit-wheel, and these also crossed the river to Pettingell's Mill.

A further mile (1.6 km) downstream stands what is left of Belton Black Mill or Long's Mill as it was also called. Probably built about 1830 it seems to have worked on into the present century although by then in a very precarious state with cracked walls encircled by iron bands. It was said that the whole structure would shake when at work to such an extent that the marshman always took an ample supply of beer to provide 'Dutch courage' while tending the mill on a windy night!

Around 1910 the owner, Mr James Lackman decided that a rebuild was necessary and this was performed by Isaac Hewitt, millwright, of Berney Arms. The old tower was taken down and used for a foundation and a new tower constructed. However the builders bricked up too steeply at first with the result that they had to bring the brickwork inwards rather sharply towards the curb giving the mill tower a distinctly convex batter.

The bricks used for the rebuild were porous and the upper brickwork thin so that water continually penetrated the tower and trickled down the walls inside

Belton Black Mill in 1938

although, from photographs of the mill in its latter days, it appears to have been given a good coating of tar. Most of the old machinery was re-used but new cap, sail-stocks with common frames and wooden upright shaft were installed. The mill was winded by a braced tailpole with windlass in the Dutch manner. The boat-shaped cap ran on a dead curb with iron centering wheels and the iron windshaft with striking-rod hole carried a small wooden clasp-arm brakewheel, with iron brake-band, meshing with a wooden wallower. The iron eight-armed pit wheel with mortised wooden cogs was driven by an iron wheel and turned an iron scoop-wheel about 14 ft (4.27 m) diameter and 7 ins (178 mm) wide with only twenty-four floats.

In 1918 Mr Harry Long bought the mill and Mr Sam Long worked it for the family. He was followed by Charlie Smith and finally by Ernie Guyton of Belton. In 1942 the sails and tailpole were dismantled and an electric pump installed. The gnarled looking tower, now bereft of tar, still stands looking rather forlorn like so many of its once proud neighbours across the river in Norfolk.

On Burgh Castle Marshes, on the south bank of Breydon Water, a mill is shown on the 1837 OS map and also, if a little inaccurately, on Bryant's map some ten years earlier. Although this mill was done away with some time near the beginning of this century it was remembered when Stanley Freese visited the area shortly before the last war. A Mr Jim Smith, with whom he spoke, had been born in one of two cottages close by the mill and remembered it as a small towermill with cloth sails, tailpole and paddle-wheel. Mr E. Snowley, then of Bradwell postmill, also confirmed that it was an old cloth-sailer.

Before we reach Gt Yarmouth and the outfall of Breydon Water one more site, at Cobholm Island, which is not an island at all now, claims our attention. This is shown on the 1837 OS map and a site to the north-east, marked by Hodskinson and Bryant, may allude to the same mill. Again this mill has been gone many years, but Mr Smith of Burgh Castle remembered it as a small, cloth-sailed towermill similar to those at Belton and Burgh Castle. In case the reader is sceptical of such personal reminiscences it should be remarked that two paintings of this mill dated *c* 1870 and 1886 exist and show it to have been as described above with clock-wise common sails carried on a wooden windshaft, a boat-shaped cap and tailpole. The mill was known as 'Black Mill' or 'Jyber's Mill'.

In Lowestoft, just north of Lake Lothing, on what was then known as Smith's Marsh the 1837 OS map shows a mill which we presume was set up for drainage purposes. By 1882 this area had been developed and the mill had disappeared.

The third area where marsh drainage mills were to be found in any quantity is

Minsmere, Eastbridge windpump; piston

known as Minsmere Level. In 1810 an Act of Parliament was obtained for draining marshland lying within the parishes of Leiston, Theberton, Dunwich, Middleton-cum-Fordley and Westleton. In 1824 a private act was passed 'for embanking and draining the level of marsh and fen-land called Minsmere Level'. This level included all the *wet land* in Theberton affected by the enclosure of the same year.

By 1844 the level was adjudged to be 'well drained and cultivated'.[13] However two years later Leiston Iron Works (Richard Garrett and Son) contracted for the better drainage of Minsmere Level by steam engine and 'succeeded in stopping those frequent inundations which had previously rendered this tract of *c* 1500 acres (600 hectares) of low, marshy land almost valueless'.[14]

Windmills also were erected in this area to assist the drainage and the gaunt remains of a few of them still lingered on until very recently. Of these the most interesting was the smock wind-pump which stood until February 1977 north of the New Cut and about half a mile (0.8 km) inland towards the hamlet of East Bridge.

This mill was only about a hundred years old but had several unusual features. With patent sails, fantail and boat-cap it was, at first glance, quite conventional until one noticed the external cant-posts and framing below the curb. These were taken from a nearby smockmill when that was blown down and added as reinforcement over the horizontal boarding of this mill by Dan England, the Ludham millwright.

The gearing and shafts were all of iron. At the lower end of the upright shaft a bevel wheel engaged a larger bevel on the end of a three-throw iron crankshaft, the other end of which was seated in a bearing mounted in the wall framing. Wooden connecting rods 4 ins (102 mm) × $3\frac{1}{2}$ in (90 mm) section and 5 ft 7 ins (1.7 m) long were coupled to pivotted guide bars and connected to the $1\frac{1}{4}$ in (32 mm) diameter × 6 ft (1.83 m) long piston rods.

The pistons were, most unusually, of square section being cast-iron 'boxes' with non-return flaps hinged at opposite sides to open in the middle. These pistons were leather bound and latterly wound in wool in an attempt to improve sealing. They ran in a zinc-lined wooden chest divided into three 1 ft (305 mm) square 'cylinders' standing about 4 ft (1.22 m) high from the ground and seated in a well. The marsh water was discharged along a wooden trough through the side of the mill into the New Cut. It was said that this arrangement was never very effective.

The mill however was very well built. Standing about 30 ft (9.15 m) high overall and carrying sails of 44 ft (13.4 m) span, the once red-painted stocks were of substantial proportions, and the cap frame was sensibly retained by means of both internal and external centering wheels both running below keep-flanges.

It was working before the last war but was damaged in 1939 and from thenceforth gradually decayed until just before its collapse, it was in a precarious state although appearing deceptively complete from a distance. Close by stands a modern iron wind-pump set up after the war to do the job of the smockmill. It still works.

Also north of the New Cut, but much nearer the coast, in what is now the Bird Sanctuary, lie the forlorn remains of another smockmill, this time of earlier origin being shown on Bryant's map and the first Ordnance Survey. It was probably put up at the time the New Cut was dug shortly after 1810 or perhaps just after the 1824 act.

Sea Wall Mill, as it is usually called, was quite different from Eastbridge Mill having wooden shafts and gears and driving a 12 ft (3.66 m) diameter × 2 ft 9 ins (840 mm) wide scoop-wheel. The all-wooden windshaft was a replacement made of oak in 1912 by Ted Friend. It carried a compass-arm brakewheel and was bored for the striking rod of the patent sails.

An interesting feature of the construction was that the sill segments were jointed over the flats of the octagon so that the feet of the cant-posts were mortised into the broadest part of each segment away from the weaker joints as is normal.

The mill was latterly tarred black but with the boat-shaped cap painted white. A guide-pole for the striking chain was provided and the mill was winded by a six-bladed fly. A replacement worm for this fly gear was cast at Norman's little foundry on Coldfair Green, Knodishall (the blacksmith's premises where a postmill stood until it was tail-winded in 1908).

This worm eventually required repairing and while it was removed the mill suffered the fate of so many others, being tail-winded in January 1935. The wooden windshaft broke clean off at the neck and the mill had finished its working life by wind.

Prior to this windpower had been supplemented by a Hupmobile petrol engine and pump but this had proved unsatisfactory and after the windmill had ceased working a diesel-powered pump was installed which was much more powerful. The mill gradually deteriorated until the decrepit remains collapsed in the summer of 1976.

About half a mile further north at Coney Hill is the reputed site of another smock drainage mill, but it appears on no map I have seen and must be dismissed until further evidence comes to light.

We must now move south of the New Cut and the Sluice to a site just to the seaward side of the ruined 'chapel' on the marshes.

Here still stand the rusting remains of an iron annular-sailed windpump which was put up in the early 1920s beside the brick foundations of a smockmill, which was itself not very old and which had blown over bodily. The cant posts from this mill were still to be seen bolted onto Eastbridge Mill as described above. From a picture postcard it is known that this mill was of slender build and tarred black with a white boat-shaped cap. Patent sails and a six-bladed fly were fitted together with a tail-pole guide for the striking chain.

The mill was reputed to have been built by Collins of Melton and drove a scoop-wheel which was retained when its successor, manufactured by John Wallis Titt of Warminster, was erected.

This iron pump is worth recording as it incorporated a weight controlled shutter mechanism with radial rods operated by bell cranks for the annular sail and was turned to wind by a six-bladed fantail with rectangular blades. The fan drove through bevels to a worm meshing with a gear wheel at the top of the braced angle leg tower. The sail of about 16 ft (4.9 m) diameter carried twenty-four canvas covered shutters.

It is not known exactly when this 'mill' stopped pumping but photographs taken in 1938 show it in good order but with an odd shutter missing from the sail. It was not galvanised but painted with bitumastic paint and for this reason has rusted badly.

A mile south of this site stood another Titt iron windpump shown on the one inch OS map of 1897 and probably dating from just before that time although again it may have had a wooden predecessor. The site lies midway between Minsmere Sluice and the hamlet of Sizewell, about 300 metres from the coast at the intersection of no less than five drainage channels.

This pump was quite different in appearance to the one just described, as its annular sail was about 25 ft (7.6 m) diameter with a solid disc at the centre about 4 ft (1.22 m) diameter from which radiated eight arms and eight stay rods. It is not certain whether these rods controlled the forty-eight shutters, each about 5 ft (1.52 m) long, although a circular control ring, connected to the centre of each shutter with a short link, was provided.

The pump was winded by a six-bladed wooden fantail and drove a scoop wheel in a wooden casing. The photograph, of 1938, shows it to be in pretty good order but it appears to have fallen into disrepair thereafter and was completely cleared away.

Another windpump is marked on the 1897 OS map, a mile and a half (2.4 km) further south, at Sizewell Hall; but it is not known whether this was of traditional type or of iron construction, though the latter seems more likely.

Moving back up the coast to Westwood Marshes, south of Walberswick, we find a little derelict red brick tower in a lovely setting surrounded by acres of gorse and broom. This mill was a picture in its working days, before the last war. With boat cap, common sails and tailpole it presented a romantic image silhouetted against the sunset and featured on several attractive picture post-cards.

The cap ran on a dead curb and the tailpole was steadied by a wooden wheel near its lower end which ran on a cement band round the tower. A winch was also provided on the end of the tailpole for pulling the cap round to wind by hitching to a series of posts as at Herringfleet mill. The iron windshaft carried a wooden

Sizewell iron windpump in 1938

Walberswick mill and marshman, Bob Westcott in 1936

brake wheel meshing with a wooden wallower on the square wooden upright shaft. At the lower end of this an iron spur wheel drove the mortise-tooth wooden pit-wheel on a wooden shaft. The iron scoop-wheel was equipped with wooden paddles. Before the first World War Jack Stannard was the marshman but he left for the war and was not seen hereabouts again. Bob Westcott succeeded him and it is he whom we see on the photograph of the mill, taken in 1936.

There are no windows in the tower, only hatches but unusually a pair of millstones was at one time installed to grind feed for horses on the estate to which the mill belonged. Bins and sack-traps were still in position after the war during which time the mill suffered grievous damage from gunnery practice. Some time after this, the breaches in the tower were patched up and the cap and sails renovated. Unfortunately in 1960 the mill was seriously damaged by a fire lit by boys and the cap, sails, brakewheel and wallower were destroyed. Restoration plans have been mooted since but to date nothing has been done.

About 300 metres due south of Walberswick marshmill, but this time in Dunwich parish, the 1897 one inch OS map shows another windpump but whether this was the small iron pump which stood recently or a predecessor is unknown.

On Reydon Marshes, near the junction of Buss Creek with the River Blyth, stands a derelict tower windpump, this being another plunger pump like the smock tower near Minsmere Eastbridge. Built about 1890, both Si Nunn of Wenhaston and Robert Martin of Beccles quoted for the job but the latter secured the contract. However the mill had an extremely short working life as, within about three or four years the sails were blown off, the windshaft breaking just behind the canister.

Blackshore Mill, as it was usually called, was fitted with patent sails, the purchase wheel for the striking chain still being in evidence as is the cap frame with outside centering wheels. The iron brakewheel, wallower, upright shaft and crown-wheels driving the three-throw crankshaft are still in position but nothing remains of the machinery below this point. Of what construction were the cylinders and pistons is open to speculation. It was said that the water pumped from the marsh drained down to a pool and thence into the nearby dyke through an underground drain or tunnel.

The mill has apparently stood looking much as it does today, since it was put out of action and one wonders why no attempt was made to reinstate it with a new windshaft. Recently however there have been moves to repair the tower which is of a soft red brick and had eroded badly particularly near the base.

Travelling southwards again we find, by the Meare or lake at Thorpeness, the postmill moved there from Aldringham (as described in Chapter 4) to take the place of a utilitarian looking iron windpump carrying storage tanks on a platform and erected only a few years previously. At Thorpeness the postmill was re-erected and a new square 'roundhouse' of concrete built with a pantiled roof. Before being put up, the main-post was drilled by auger for the pump rod. The pump drive was taken from the wallower to the upright shaft, on the bottom of which is a bevel wheel driving a horizontal shaft carrying a crank-disc from which a connecting rod runs to the long vertical pump rod. The pump served to lift water from an artesian bore to the nearby water tower known as the 'House in the Clouds' and which used to serve the houses on the Thorpeness Estate. The water, which given a steady wind, was said to flow at the rate of 1800 gallons (8200 litres) per hour was conveyed to the water tower by an underground pipe.

The mill worked until about the outbreak of the last war and was still in fair condition, but with sail shutters removed, after the war. Since then the mill has been preserved by the proprietors of the Thorpeness Estate.

A mile (1.6 km) from Thorpeness beside the coast road to Aldeburgh, next to Halfway House, one can still discern some octagonal foundations about 16 ft (4.88 m) over the flats and with walls 13½ ins (343 mm) thick. This was the base of the Black Mill mentioned in chapter 4. From a photograph we know it to have carried the usual patent sails and six-bladed fly. It was demolished *c* 1900 when an automatic sluice was installed.

Also at Aldeburgh, just south-west of the town at a site called Mill Piece stood a small black postmill marked by the Ipswich engineer, Peter Bruff, on a plan of 1851 showing proposed improvements for draining the marsh. Nothing more is known of this mill; presumably it was a 'hollow postmill' but whether driving a scoop-wheel or plunger pump is anyone's guess. It is believed to have gone by the turn of the century and may even have been a corn mill.

South west of this site, on Aldeburgh Corporation Marshes and near the north bank of the River Alde, stood Pettit's Mill, a smock drainage mill said to have been working in 1897.[3]

From Aldeburgh we must travel down the coast to the Orford area before we find any more drainage mills. It was from this district that the tiny postmill buck, which finished up at Saxtead Green, was reputed to have come.

To the west of Orford, near the Butley River and Chillesford Lodge, stood a nice little red brick towermill with boat cap, fantail and scoop-wheel. This is shown on the 1837 OS map and may be the site shown, possibly erroneously, by Bryant about half a mile (0.8 km) nearer Orford.

This rather inaccessible mill had obviously been heightened at some time as the upper portion of the tower had vertical walls. If originally the tower stood only as high as the tapered portion then it would have been very short indeed. The striking chain for the patent sails was prevented from swinging against the tower by a braced guide pole. The cap ran on six travelling wheels and was centred by four wheels running inside the curb. The brakewheel, wallower and upright-shaft were all wooden. An iron crown-wheel, at the lower end of the large upright shaft, drove the eight-armed, two-piece mortised pit-wheel 8 ft (2.44 m) in diameter. A wooden wheel shaft carried the 10 ft 6 ins (3.2 m) diameter iron scoop-wheel with wooden floats.

This mill was working up until about the outbreak of the last war. It thereafter fell into decay until, in the 1950s, it was completely repaired only to be wrecked in a gale in the winter of 1958–59. When I last tramped over the marshes in July 1967 to see what was left I found the tower pulled down to within 7 ft (2.14 m) of the ground and bits of the machinery lying in the grass.

Actually in Leiston town there stood a tower windpump but this had nothing to do with marsh drainage as it was constructed to supply water to the house of Mr Richard Garrett (of traction engine fame). This mill is shown on the 1881 six inch OS map but nothing much is known about it except that the tower, sails and fly were all painted bright red.

Two other windpumps in this part of the county are known and both graced the attractive seaside town of Southwold.

One was an annular-sailed iron pump with large, eight-armed sail carrying forty-eight shutters and a six-bladed fly. This was erected around 1886 on top of the water tower which still stands on Southwold Common. It was probably by Titt of Warminster and used to lift water from a well into the iron cistern which held 40000 gallons (182000 litres) of water. A photograph taken from the lighthouse in 1893 shows this pump together with the Black Postmill, and in the distance, the brick windpump on Reydon marshes.

Southwold windpump and Black Mill

Southwold saltworks and windpump

The other pump was connected with the salt works which were established at the southern end of the town in 1660.[15] They were situated at the head of a creek up which water flowed into a well over which stood this small windpump. It was of the hollow-post type with cloth sails winded by a vane. The plunger pump lifted the water from the well into a trough which spanned the road alongside and carried it to the evaporating pans.

Early this century the business was sold to the Southwold and London Trading Company. Apparently it was possible to make a profit on fine table salt but for coarse salt the company could not compete with big firms elsewhere. However, rock salt was brought from Cheshire to Southwold for refining and latterly salt-water baths were added to the business. A second trough from the windpump conveyed water to the bath-houses nearby.

The business closed down many years ago but the windpump, largely constructed of wood, lingered on, with two sail-frames until at least 1938. The clockwise sails were mounted on an iron cross which carried the square tubular sail-arms. The sail-frames, which were no more than 6 ft (1.83 m) long, comprised inner and outer transverse bars with four iron rods between them. There was an iron brake, chain operated, which contracted on a brake-drum in front of the tiny head wheel. Also in evidence was a handle for operating the pump in calm weather. Nothing now remains of this quaint relic.

At Bury St Edmunds corporation waterworks, in 1899 or 1900, J. W. Titt constructed a large iron pump on top of a brick tower, rather like that described in Southwold. This one was known as the Simplex model and boasted an annular sail 40 ft (12.2 m) diameter carried on ten arms and with fifty shutters. These were connected with an annular ring about one third of their length from the outside of the 12 ft (3.66 m) long shutters. A bowsprit carried ten strainer wires to the peripheral ring of the sail and also five control bars to effect opening and closing the shutters.

Two large, eight-bladed fantails were employed and the whole construction stood 81 ft (24.7 m) high over the sail. It is said to have cost £550. An advertisement of Titt's dated 1906 states that the Simplex Geared Wind Engine was built 'in all sizes, from 18 ft (4.94 m) to 50 ft (15.25 m) in diameter.' A photograph of 1911 shows the Bury pump in use but exactly when it ceased functioning is uncertain. It is said the remains of it were cleared away in about 1940 probably for scrap to aid the war effort. A second Titt Simplex engine was erected by the Bury Corporation at the Sewage works about 1898.

An early photograph of Gt Cornard watermill[16] on the River Stour, south-east of Sudbury, shows a small hollow postmill with common sails and tailpole standing close by the watermill building. The structure stood perhaps 12 ft (3.66 m) high and might be dismissed as a 'garden ornament' were it not for the fact that a member of the Baker family (who still have the watermill) told Stanley

Freese, before the last war, that a small windpump had worked in the area. The site described then was on marshy ground $\frac{3}{4}$ mile (1.2 km) further to the south-east. The 1884 six inch OS map shows a windpump at this location and one wonders if the little structure in the photograph was moved to the second site. However it is believed that this pump was of smock type.

Mr Baker told Stanley Freese that the sails of this little mill became unsafe so were shortened but the mill then would not work properly so was pulled down. This would have been in about 1905 although OS maps until *c* 1920 mark a pump at this site.

Looking through the above notes it seems likely that in a few years, and with the exception of a handful of preserved examples, very little will remain of the marsh-drainage and pumping mills of Suffolk. Norfolk still has many remains of Broadland drainage towermills standing but the majority of these are crumbling, and except for those preserved as amenities, it is probable that soon the remainder will stand only as gaunt capless and sail-less towers.

Framsden postmill, with sails turning on 8 Feb. 1970

6

Preservation and the Future

Rex Wailes said to me that he felt no sadness at the passing of so many windmills, but gladness that he had been interested enough to visit and examine them during a period when they were still relatively common. Stanley Freese, 'Sid' Simmons and other of their contemporaries were also fortunate in being born at a time which allowed their youthful enthusiasm to be deployed in seeking out and recording many fine and interesting mills.

Enthusiasts today must find 'mill hunting' a somewhat less rewarding hobby, and some turn their energies to trying to restore and preserve a little of what is left. In this way future generations will still be able to visit a few of the old windmills and learn how their antecedents ground wheat to make flour or, as forerunners of the modern engineer, built and maintained these quaint, but ingenious machines.

Windmill preservation is not such a new thing as we might suppose. Edward Fitzgerald, the poet (1809–83), bought some land at Woodbridge in order to save a windmill thereon which otherwise would have been pulled down. Around 1925 the owner of the postmill at Halesworth started demolition. Mr Scrimgeour of nearby Wissett Hall objected to this as it spoilt his view so he paid Robert Martin of Beccles to repair it. This was effected using parts taken from Topcroft postmill in Norfolk in 1933. The upper part of the buck and machinery were renewed and a single pair of stones set up on the left side of the buck. The great spurwheel was unusual in having seven arms. Unfortunately, the mill was to enjoy only a short resurrection as, when Mr Scrimgeour died in 1937, the fly and sail shutters were removed and by degrees the mill was done away with.

The postmill at Stanton might not still be standing but for restoration work carried out at the outbreak of the second war. The mill was disused by 1918 and was becoming dilapidated in 1937 when Rex Wailes inspected it for the SPAB and reported its condition. The Society, considering it worthy of attention, launched an appeal for funds during 1938 and the following year Amos Clarke commenced repairs. Hunts of Soham also worked on the mill, the cost of around £600 being a considerable sum then. Work included replacement of the left side girt—no mean task, rebuilding the winding tackle using the original wheels and gears, and new boarding. Unfortunately the tailstones were removed and their remains can still be seen leaning against the roundhouse wall. The roundhouse roof was rebuilt and the late William Bryant, brother of John Bryant of Pakenham, remembered the millwright sawing down the length of each board to form the requisite taper. It was planned to fit the iron windshaft from Wickhambrook Great Mill and a second pair of sails. Alas, with the outbreak of war this was never done, and the sails remained unfinished in the yard.

With roof covered with sheet-iron and timbers painted grey, presumably to lessen its visibility as a landmark for enemy aircraft, the mill worked again for a while with two sails. However, by 1946 Mr Bryant had given up using the mill as it was not proving worthwhile. The mill, with sailframes cut down to six bays, gradually deteriorated again until, by 1969, Mr Bryant was worried that the fly and its posts would fall back onto his nearby buildings. So Chris Hullcoop, that champion of Suffolk mills, together with Philip Lennard, from Essex, carefully removed the eight blades of the fly.

Stanton now is a large village with industries and a new primary school opposite the mill. Surely this growth should produce the interest and drive required to ensure the mill's preservation. There are plans to use the roundhouse as a craft workshop. Failing its preservation on site it would be a good candidate for moving to the Abbott's Hall Museum at Stowmarket where it is hoped to erect examples of the various mill types and where a good start has been made with Alton watermill, rescued from the clutches of the Tattingstone reservoir.

Perhaps the most spectacular restoration scheme in Suffolk was that undertaken at Saxtead Green mill. The mill had ground grist until 1947 and in 1951 Mr S. C. Sullivan, son-in-law of the last miller, Mr A. S. Aldred, placed it in the guardianship of the Ministry of Works (now the DOE).

Jesse Wightman, who had assisted Mr Aldred in maintaining the mill during the previous thirty years, acted as adviser to the Ministry and during the years of restoration, from 1957 until 1960, undertook several of the major tasks himself. The mill was surrounded by scaffolding, the sails were removed, the windshaft lowered and the buck dismantled.

The crowntree from the recently demolished Wetheringsett mill, which was wider, was shortened and placed on the original corsetted post and the buck was entirely re-framed with larger windows to admit plenty of light for the thousands of visitors, who would swarm to this superb example of the millwright's art each year. A brand new oak brakewheel was built and fitted by Wightman and the only pity was that the original wheel was left standing outside to gradually rot. In 1971 a new stock and one sail were fitted and in 1978 futher work on the sails was carried out.

To help protect the mill after the very costly restoration an elaborate lightning conductor was provided. To cope with turning to wind a slipper at the bottom of the step bears on an earthed copper ring set in the wooden tramway. Although not working now, Mr Sullivan often releases the brake and allows the sails, now fitted with a small complement of shutters, to idle round in the breeze.

To their lasting credit the East Suffolk County Council, as it then was, made the decision in 1948 to try to preserve one of each of the main types of windmill. They helped towards the cost of rebuilding Saxtead Green mill and in 1950 acquired the leasehold of Buttrum's towermill in Burkitt Road, Woodbridge.

In 1954 this mill was put into good repair for a sum of just under £4,000, the Pilgrim Trust assisting the County Council towards the cost. Messrs Thomas Smithdale & Sons, the Norfolk millwrights, carried out the work, building a new cap and replacing the rusty iron-railed decorative gallery with a less attractive looking wooden one. In December 1966 the mill was damaged in a gale, necessitating the fly being repaired. In 1970 a further £500 was spent on essential repairs, including work on one stock, but early in 1973 a new pitch pine stock was hoisted into position and a new sailframe fitted.

As an example of a smockmill the County Council chose to maintain Herringfleet drainage mill. Some £500 was spent on repairs, Smithdale & Sons again carrying out the work. Half the cost was contributed by the Ministry of Works and the remainder mostly by the Council who received small contributions from other interested bodies. The mill was officially handed over to the care of the County Council on 25 July 1958.[1]

Charlie Howlett, the last marshman, was retained as caretaker but after his retirement the mill sails seldom turned. However, in Peter Dolman, a County Council employee and mill enthusiast, living at Ipswich, the mill has found a new champion as two or three times a year an 'open day' is held and Peter and one or two friends winch the cap round into the wind and spread the cloths so that, wind permitting, the sails can turn, driving the scoop-wheel and pumping water if the dyke is full. Few of the broadland holidaymakers, cruising by on the River Waveney, can realise they are seeing the only workable full-sized drainage mill in Britain on one of the few days it is in action.

Unfortunately while some mills were being saved, others were falling into such disrepair that the cost of restoring them was becoming prohibitive. It is a sad but true fact that only so much money is available for these projects and the selection of suitable candidates becomes a difficult matter. Several factors have to be considered such as condition, historical importance of machinery, accessibility and—most important of all—the interest of the owner.

Since the last war several mills have collapsed or been pulled down, Debenham towermill being unnecessarily butchered in December 1962 as was Westleton postmill in the following summer. An effort to convert Barnham towermill into a house in 1967 deprived the mill of its interesting and elegant machinery but since that date the Civic Amenities Act has served to better protect those reasonably complete mills remaining, most of which are grade 2 listed buildings.

Freckenham smockmill was in a very poor state when cleared away in 1967 but Gt Thurlow smockmill, also in the extreme west of the county, suffered a happier fate. This mill, which had lost its sails and fly in 1920 and subsequently its cap, was on the estate purchased by Mr R. A. Vestey, a wealthy businessman. Around 1960 he decided to have the mill restored as a visual amenity and Mr Frank Farrow, who now owns Dalham smockmill, was asked to advise on the repairs.

During 1962 Messrs Rooks, builders of Haverhill, carried out the work, which was extensive, comprising a new cap clad in two layers of marine quality plywood covered with roofing felt, new sheers and fly framing, stocks and sailframes and horizontal weatherboarding like the original but tarred black. In the interim years the mill had been boarded vertically over the original boards. The cap was not arranged to turn nor was the fly geared to the curb. The keen observer will notice that the fly blades have been fitted with an excessive 'angle of weather' due to the slots in the spokes being cut in the wrong direction, necessitating the spokes being turned through ninety degrees to try and rectify the fault. In January 1976 a sail suffered gale damage and was consequently removed for repair.

Mr John Bryant, whose family had owned Pakenham towermill since 1885, had always kept his mill in good repair using the services of millwright Amos Clarke. When the mill needed a new stock in 1950 one was procured from the derelict Thurston postmill and installed by Clarke and his son, Alf. While this was being done it was found that the weather-beam was rotten. A new beam of African oak was cut to shape with an adze and it was then found that the old neck bearing was also unserviceable. A happy solution was found with the installation of the swing-pot and neck-brass which had been taken out of Buxhall towermill when that suffered severe gale damage many years previously.[2] New sails were also fitted and it was around this time also that Mr Bryant had Clarke build the wooden cap gallery which was patterned on that of Wendover mill in Buckinghamshire.

In 1960, Mr Bryant reported to the County Planning Officer that his mill was now in urgent need of major repair work. He also contacted the SPAB for advice. The Ministry of Works then agreed to make a grant of £750 if the County Council would grant a similar amount. Jesse Wightman was asked by the County Council to carry out a detailed examination of the mill to ensure that any repair work was comprehensive. He estimated that the total cost of restoration would be not less than £4,000.

Early in 1961 both the County Council and Ministry of Works agreed to make grants of £2,000 each towards repair work, any sum above this amount being the owner's responsibility. The Ministry stipulated that their contribution was conditional upon Mr Bryant and his family continuing to work the mill.[3]

The ensuing repair work was fairly comprehensive. Amos Clarke had died in 1953 and the job was entrusted to R. Thompson & Son of Alford, Lincolnshire. The old copper covered cap was re-framed and clad in aluminium sheeting which should require no maintenance. The work was carried out during the summer of 1963 and included the provision of new stock and two new sails. The fantail was also extensively rebuilt.

In October of the same year the mill was opened to the public and was worked occasionally without a serious hitch until June 1971 when lightning struck, splitting one stock and badly damaging a sail. The sack chain, which reached nearly to the ground, was broken in four places but saved the mill from complete destruction by fire. After the damage was rectified Mr Bryant had a lightning conductor installed which, hopefully, will prevent a recurrence.

Stanley Freese had hopes that the little marsh mill south of Walberswick would be put back into repair after it had been wantonly damaged by fire in 1960. It had been repaired a few years previously but its remote marshland location makes it vulnerable and to date no scheme for its restoration has been proposed.

St Olaves marshmill has also suffered from vandalism, but here something has been achieved. As far back as 1960 a Mill Preservation Committee had been formed and had raised sufficient funds to pay for two new sails. A few years later the older pair of sails fell off and it was feared the mill might be doomed. However Chris Hullcoop had been approached by the sole surviving member of the committee, Mr J. F. Miller. He sent a report to the East Suffolk County Council and the Suffolk Preservation Society, who obtained an estimate of the cost of restoration. In 1970 the East Suffolk Planning Committee approved a grant of £100 towards the cost of repairs. Further money was raised but the mill had to wait until the winter of 1974–75 for work to be commenced. By then it had been badly vandalised and Philip Lennard, the millwright, 'rebuilt it like a battleship' to use his own words, to combat further wilful damage.

The postmill windpump at Thorpeness has been mentioned in chapter 4. Belonging to Thorpeness Estate Ltd, which had endeavoured to keep the mill in good repair, it had nevertheless deteriorated considerably by 1973, necessitating props being inserted through the roundhouse roof. In September of that year the mill had a lucky escape when the surrounding heath caught fire and burnt one sail and stock.

The following year the newly formed Suffolk Coastal Council considered the matter of a grant towards the cost of repairs but a decision was deferred. By 1975 the mill was in urgent need of attention and a new millwright had appeared on the scene. David Nicholls of Jameson Marshall Ltd, who already had considerable experience in millwrighting, estimated that the repairs would cost about £9,600, and once more the matter came before the Council Planning Committee. It was agreed to recommend to the Policy and Resources Committee that the council meet the cost of one third of the work up to a maximum of £3,500 provided it made the mill capable of working. The owners would also pay a third and the Heritage Coast Officer recommended the Countryside Commission to meet the remainder. During 1976 and 1977 the mill was completely restored and is now owned by the County Council who have opened a Tourist Information Centre in the roundhouse. It is hoped that this unique postmill pump will long grace the village resort.

The only other drainage mill, which it was hoped to preserve, suffered the fate of being restored too well! Frank Blake, a seventy-seven year old engineer and millwright, came out of retirement in 1952 to work for Mr Alistair Watson, owner of the marshes at Orford on which stood the so-called Chillesford Lodge marshmill. Despite his years Mr Blake worked up to 100 hours a week for no less than three years to bring the derelict mill back to full working order. He lived in the mill during this time with, it was said, the *Times Literary Supplement* and rats as his only companions![4]

The work involved fitting a new scoop-wheel, re-cogging other wheels and making cap, sails and fly. This is where he came unstuck for the sails were fitted with a full complement of shutters and the fly was of large dimensions for so small a mill. It looked splendid in its new finery, but not for long! In the winter of 1958–59 the sails and fly were blown off and thereafter the cap, so reducing the proud little lady to worse than her previous dereliction.

The problem here was that a working (or fully workable) mill needs to be closely attended. The dangers of being 'tail-winded' have been described at length in chapter 4. If a mill is to wind itself then it is important that the winding gears and bearings be regularly inspected and greased. Bearing in mind the extremely exposed and isolated position and the absence of the full attention of a marshman it would have been safer to fit only half the shutters and a smaller, more open bladed fly. This would have left plenty of power to work the mill in a good wind.

Gracing a wooded eminence, Holton St Peter postmill has been a landmark for well over two hundred years. It went out of use about the turn of this century, and was shortly afterwards stripped of its machinery. Thereafter it was used as a sort of summerhouse with the addition of a viewing platform high up at the back of the buck with access from a door at top floor level. At about the same time the mill was equipped with a fantail but was later without one for a while until the present large fly was fitted by Robert Martin in 1938. The mill was allowed to wind itself and attempts were made to keep it in reasonable order.

In the early 1950s the SPS supplied paint for the mill but by 1960 the elderly owner, Colonel T. S. Irwin, realised that more extensive renovation was required. An appeal for funds was issued about this time and Col. Irwin stood as Chairman of the Restoration Fund Committee which had been formed as far back as 1951. Discussions were started with the ESCC and the Suffolk

Preservation Society but at this stage these bodies could not see their way clear to help.[5]

However in 1963 volunteers commenced work. These were Mr and Mrs H. J. Fisk of Reydon, Marcus Cook and Chris Hullcoop of whom we have heard already and will hear more anon. Initially the mill was given a coat of paint provided by the Paint Division of ICI Ltd. Meanwhile the East Suffolk County Planning Committee had been approached by the SPAB with regard to the provision of a small grant to enable the voluntary workers to continue their efforts. The following year Stanley Freese came from Buckinghamshire to retire at nearby Wenhaston. He soon learnt of the work being done at Holton and offered his services.

The fly, which was unbalanced, and so out of true that it often struck one fly post, had to be repaired and adjusted. It was then decided that the outer pair of (spring) sails were unsafe and would have to be dismantled without delay. Next it was found that, when hand cranked, the worm gears in the fly drive were binding at every other revolution. This appeared to be because one of the tram wheels had never been locked properly on its spindle after it had broken in halves at some time when the wind had caught the mill side on, lifting the wheel which then crashed down onto the concrete track. This seems a likely explanation as the wheels on this mill are mounted very close together under the step strings. The fault was rectified and all the shaft bearings trued up and tightened.

Shortly after this Neville Martin, the millwright, called to inspect the mill for the Ministry of Works. Meanwhile the buck roof had been covered with a tarpaulin and the structure reinforced by the addition of an oak cantilever beam on the bottom floor from the front of the post to beneath a new prick-post fitted behind the original one. This was necessitated by the mill having been lengthened at the head by bolting rather inadequate extensions to the sheer trees. The new subsidiary prick-post was continued on the floor above to the underside of the very broad weather-beam and the load supported through the cantilevered beam onto a transverse timber placed across the front ends of the main sheers.

An incident around this time serves to illustrate one of the hazards which may confront the mill owner and restorer. In Stanley Freese's own words:

All went well until, on March 31st 1965 the Colonel arrived at my cottage in haste to announce that the fly was whizzing round out of control and would I come immediately to help as it had been interfered with!

We hurried there and found the fly uncoupled, the gears wedged and a stone placed in front of the tram wheels. Watching the fly I saw that the wind was rising and falling as it always does in Suffolk, and the fan being so low over the stairs that one had to duck under it, I was able to grab at the iron rods between the vanes as they passed in a lull until the fly could be held still. It was then fairly easy to couple up the drive and set the mill turning to wind again. Such is life!

Early in 1966 the two remaining common sails were repaired and sail cloths, dyed the traditional red ochre, were made. They saw some service in late 1965 and in 1966 and on one glorious, fine windy day the sails turned non-stop from morning to dusk—a fine sight! Consideration was given to fitting four new sails but Rex Wailes, representing the Ministry of Works, disapproved on the grounds of excessive strain on the head of the mill.

By this time the East Suffolk Planning Committee had agreed in principle to help financially. It was estimated that it would cost £1,240 to repair the mill thoroughly and the Historic Buildings Council stated that they were prepared to make a grant provided that the County Council made a similar contribution and that the restored mill was opened to the public. It was stated that although the County Council had already taken steps to preserve three typical windmills, it felt justified in making a contribution towards the preservation of this one, particularly in view of the voluntary efforts made to repair it.[6]

During 1966 Neville Martin of Beccles commenced repairs which were to include a complete new buck roof, reboarding the rest of the buck, work on the floors, strengthening of the step strings and the fitting of four new sails. These sails were constructed with light common frames and hollow, prefabricated stocks to lessen the strain on the ancient structure. It is a pity that now they cannot turn for fear of straining the glued joints of the stocks.

The restoration extended over two years, but finally, in March 1968 the work was completed and maintenance was assured for another fifty years as the County Council took a lease on the mill for that period. The mill is now opened to the public on certain weekends of the year and may be viewed by appointment at other times.

The mill restoration scheme with which I have been most closely associated was that commenced in June 1966 at Framsden. The mill had gradually been deteriorating and recently the front stock had broken in the centre, half the stock and one sail falling, leaving the other half-stock and sail hanging on the striking rod. When I arrived to offer my services, I found Chris Hullcoop already at work with Vincent Pargeter and Peter Stenning. The head boarding had been removed and some re-framing was in progress. My first 'millwrighting' job was painting a pile of weatherboards with paint kindly given by ICI Ltd.

An interesting fact concerning the head of Framsden mill was that it had originally borne a sharp pointed 'prow' but the bottom rail, conforming to this profile, had later been overlaid to give the mill the typical late Suffolk curved head line. The buck roof was overlain with hardboard and this covered with two layers of roofing felt, practical if a little inelegant, very cheap, quick to fit and easy to maintain. Apart from gifts of paint and other materials £50 had been given by

Demolition of Earl Soham postmill in 1947   *Framsden postmill at start of restoration in 1966*

Lord Tollemache of nearby Helmingham and £50 each by the ESCC and SPS.

Next, the left side of the buck was dealt with, the bottom side rail being overlaid with a new piece of timber and window frames, diagonal braces and studding being replaced as required. Long studs, whose end joints had rotted, were shortened and used to replace shorter studs, thus requiring less new timber. To facilitate the work scaffolding platforms were cantilevered out from the side of the mill and repositioned at various levels as work progressed. All this was happening in 1966, and during that first year Frank Farrow and Stanley Freese were helping with the work. At this stage it was not intended to fully reboard the buck, so that the tail boarding and part of the right hand side was painted. A new fly string was fitted on the right-hand side as the original one was rotten.

Eyebolts were fixed through the upper rail on the finished (left-hand) side to facilitate maintenance and an unusual feature, advocated by Chris was the provision of a felt covered 'drip board' sloping out from under the eave to throw rainwater away from the side of the buck.

In the following year more was achieved, a local farmer's son, Nigel Foulger, now helping us. It must be remembered that virtually all the 'on site' work was carried out at weekends although Chris spent part of his holidays there and also continued preparatory work away from the mill during the week.

The post at Framsden is relatively small in section and badly split. Although probably adequate for a mill turning to wind we felt unhappy about the stresses incurred with the wind able to act on the greater area of the side of the buck and in this situation the steps are no longer capable of helping to resist the thrust. In this dilemma we were helped by the engineering firm for which I work, who kindly manufactured a set of substantial longitudinal bars and steel hoops which we screwed and clamped around the ailing post. The bars came only to bottom floor level but we later extended four of them past the shoulder of the post to further strengthen it. If the mill were ever to turn to wind again the reinforcement could be removed or easily modified.

We also tilted the buck slightly as it was decidedly 'head-sick' and also leaning to the right, the latter no doubt due to the action of the heavy sails turning in that direction. Tilting was achieved by removing the wood-wears around the post and levering the buck over with a 6 ft (1.83 m) crowbar extended to about 10 ft (3 m) with a length of scaffold pole. It was still an arduous task! The wood-wears were then adjusted and re-fitted. We found that as well as leaning the right hand side was moving away from the left at eaves level so to stop this trend we inserted steel tie-rods from wall to wall.

By August we were stripping the right hand side of boards as by now the owner, Mr Stanley Ablett and his son John, were holding 'open weekends' at the Bank Holidays to attract funds and our plans were growing more ambitious. Stanley Freese was still visiting the mill but by then his health was beginning to deteriorate and it was at this time that Chris suggested that he might like to take up his survey of Suffolk windmills again, this time with myself as collaborator.

When we uncovered the right-hand side girt we found, to our amazement, that it was completely broken through above the crown tree. It is a testimony to the generous safety margins allowed for empirically by the old-time millwrights that, despite the failure of this major structural member, no disastrous collapse had occurred; although this item had doubtless contributed to the mill being 'down' at the front, right-hand corner. We could not reduce the sag but hopefully stopped further movement by bolting a heavy angle iron on top of the girt to take the tension load.

We also experimented on this side by lining the weatherboards with a layer of exterior-quality hardboard but it will be many years before we know if this 'second line of defence' has any practical value. As winter approached we struggled on with the boarding but handling 17 ft (5.2 m) long weatherboards on a narrow scaffold platform in a near-blizzard was no joke, and we finally desisted to await better weather.

The Spring of 1968 saw work nearing completion on the side. About this time we were joined by Adrian Colman, then only fourteen, who worked steadfastly with us for several years until forced to leave for the best of reasons: he had bought the post mill at Garboldisham, Norfolk and started repairs. By summer the two sails had been lowered for repair. The stock was in fair condition but we reinforced its centre by fitting clamps, the traditional way of strengthening an ailing stock.

Inside the mill we turned our attention to the stones. We decided to set up the left-hand 4 ft (1.22 m) diameter pair to full working order; they were lighter, newer and in better condition than the 4 ft 6 in (1.37 m) right-hand pair, whose runner we placed in the tail of the buck to help balance and also to show the stone faces exposed. We had to replace the flooring at the rear of the stone floor, as a gaping hole attested to the erstwhile position of the flour dresser, removed some years previously. The tentering gear was also refurbished and the stone nut re-cogged using apple-wood from some old standard trees given by a local farmer.

1969 saw the brake dismantled and repaired. Two of the elm segments were rotten so we replaced them and new curved, mild steel ties were fashioned to join the segments. Although the remaining segments had worn quite thin, we considered the re-built brake adequate for the limited use to which it was going to be put.

In March the first, refurbished sail frame was hoisted and by late July the second one followed. A small complement of shutters was fitted, most of them using existing frames, where they would fit, but a few being made from scratch by a ninety-odd year old helper, Max Defatch. The frames were covered, not with the traditional white lead soaked canvas, but with 16 gauge (1.6 mm) aluminium sheet. Drain holes were drilled in the corners to prevent water lodging when the shutters were opened.

Meanwhile the striking gear was put in order, the original cross which was broken being replaced with that from the collapsed Eye postmill; and to help prevent rust streaks on the buck the pivot bolts were made from stainless steel. Lastly that year, boards for re-cladding the tail of the mill were being prepared, for fitting at a later date.

1970 heralded the end of work on the two remaining sails, it being decided that the replacement of the outer pair, as well as being a formidable task, would impose an excessive strain on the frail old structure which, in fairness, had never been built with the intention of carrying large and heavy patent sails. Imagine our joy when, on February 7th, the sails turned in a fresh westerly breeze for the first time in about 35 years.

In view of the fact that the mill stands on high ground with few trees of any height nearby we had been considering the desirability of fitting a lightning conductor and to this end procured the relevant British Code of Practice.[7] In one respect it was fortunate that Framsden mill no longer turns to wind as the provision of a movable connection to earth, as is fitted at Saxtead mill, was not necessary here. We decided to use commercially pure aluminium strip which is much cheaper than copper, is easy to fit and leaves no green streaks. The conductor runs from the sail tips to the windshaft canister to which it is bolted. As the neck bearing is wood (and not brass as at Saxtead) contact is made by a heavily weighted slipper block bearing on the neck of the shaft from which the conductor runs via the outside steps to a copper earthing rod. Conductors at front and rear of the buck roof are also connected into the system. We have no evidence of a lightning strike since the conductor was fitted, so cannot really comment on its efficacy but I felt that a somewhat detailed description might be of help to any aspiring mill restorer.

During the spring of that year work on setting up the left-hand (4 ft—1.22 m) pair of stones progressed. The runner stone, which for years had lain on the floor against the left-hand side-grit, was re-positioned and it was then that we discovered the inscription and date 1794 (see also chapter 2).

By May a platform had been erected at the tail of the buck and the rest of that summer was spent in repairing the framing, fitting a new window frame in the rear gable and reboarding. It was noted that the rear gable framing was extremely crude, possibly the work of the miller at the time the tail was extended, and not what one would expect of any self-respecting millwright! An interesting discovery, uncovered with the removal of the boarding, was the material used for the left-hand extension corner post. This was no less than a length of common sail whip with a piece of oak sailbar still in position in one of the mortises. You never know what you are going to find when repairing an old mill!

As winter approached the fear that the fly might blow away prompted us to remove it for safe keeping as after nearly forty years of neglect the fly posts were extremely rotten in places. Hopefully one day they will be refitted but that day has not yet come.

During the winter Chris worked on replacing the brakewheel cogs, using hornbeam from a tree blown down on the Shrubland Estate. The work was made easier by the fact that the cogs were mortised into oak segments which could be unbolted from the wheel. In the original wheel are square mortises for sixty-one widely spaced cogs and the segments, with seventy-eight cogs, had doubtless been added at the time the iron wallower was fitted and the two pairs of stones set up in the head. This arrangement enabled Chris to take home the segments and work on re-cogging them throughout the winter without the necessity of motor-cycling the 21 miles (33 km) to and from the mill every weekend.

Nevertheless it was an exacting task; the hypoidal cogs, each angled in relation to its mortise, occupied around 300 hours work.

The following May saw the segments assembled on the brakewheel again, some cogs having to be fitted at the intersection of the segments once these were firmly in position. Next the governor was repaired, the left-hand stones set up with vat, horse and shoe from an old power-mill and lastly a new bell alarm firmly riveted in position (to balk souvenir hunters).

The mill was now in a fit state to do some 'rough grinding' with a strong

out the strain on the stock but they seldom turn in the wind and since that memorable day back in 1972 no flour has trickled from the stones and down the meal spout to a waiting sack.

It will be seen that several attempts at restoration have been blessed with success due to a combination of propitious circumstances. Other mills, some no less deserving of survival, have failed to endure due to the lack of one or more essential ingredient. These include the postmills at Earl Soham, Parham, Woolpit and Westhall, Blundeston towermill and the smockmills at Alderton and Wortham.

Sometimes even the efforts of the demolishers are scotched. This was so in the autumn of 1963 when the Ministry of Housing and Local Government had agreed to the demolition of the ailing postmill at Woolpit. The mill had been photographically recorded and Chris Hullcoop, who at that time was working on Holton mill, had been offered any parts he thought he could use on that project. He arrived at Woolpit one morning to start dismantling the machinery only to find that that old friend and foe of windmills, the wind, had beaten him to the job by a few hours.

Friston postmill also narrowly escaped the hands of the demolition contractor in 1970 when the owner and last miller, Mr Caleb Reynolds Wright, fearful of the mill's condition, applied for permission to have it pulled down.[8] This fine large mill had been earmarked by the ESCC as early as 1939 for retention with a handful of others and had continued to work intermittently with an electric motor for another twenty years. Mr Wright removed the stones in 1962 and the mill, although still able to wind itself, gradually deteriorated. In 1965 an application to demolish was approved by the County Planning Committee and sanctioned by the Minister of Housing as was required by law. For various reasons demolition work was not put in hand and in 1968 changes in planning regulations made it necessary to go through the whole procedure again if it was wished to pull the mill down.

Villagers, who were questioned, seemed equally divided as to whether the mill should be demolished or retained and a lively debate on the mill's future ensued in the local newspapers. The County Planning Committee called for a millwright's report and deferred its decision for one month to give interested local people an opportunity to organise an appeal.

Some enthusiasts felt that the mill might be dismantled and removed to the Rural Life Museum at Stowmarket but most of the local objections to demolition rested on the mill's importance to the village scene which it had dominated for more than 150 years. When the County Planning Committee sat again the solution of moving the mill to the museum was agreed in principle. The millwright's report stated that the mill's condition was better than expected, that the main timbers were sound and that there was little or no fear of it collapsing. The curator of the museum said that he would be pleased to have the mill there as long term plans included a site for a postmill, financial help was promised by a number of people and the future of Friston mill, albeit at a new site, seemed assured.[9]

However, this was not to be its fate. Early in 1971 an anonymous benefactor offered, in conjunction with a local fund-raising scheme, to ensure the restoration of the mill on its present site subject to the County Council accepting the responsibility for subsequent maintenance. Mr Wright died the following year, aged 86, and the mill and house were purchased by Mr Piers Hartley who intends to restore the mill to its former splendour.

With grants made by the County Council and other donations the mill fund grew steadily and eventually in 1977 Messrs Jameson Marshall started work, replacing the roundhouse roof and completely restoring the buck but leaving the mill without sails awaiting further funds to enable the job to continue.

One other postmill still in urgent need of major repair is the little one at Syleham, owned by Mr Ivor Wingfield, who has expressed a wish to repair the mill and has carried out a little remedial work.

The oldest postmill in the county at Drinkstone has been kept standing by the efforts of Mr Wilfred Clover, the miller, but how long it will continue to grace the scene without major attention is very uncertain.

It is still hoped to preserve the fine smockmill at Dalham which was purchased by Mr Frank Farrow in 1970 on his retirement. This mill had already been repaired in 1961 when the fly was removed and the cap and tower clad in roofing felt. There is no doubt that these timely repairs have kept most of the weather from penetrating the mill so that it is still in relatively good order despite several bad cant-posts and rot in the brakewheel.

Frank Farrow has for many years maintained a deep interest in windmills, his uncle having been the last miller at Gt Wratting smockmill in Cambridgeshire in the 1920s. In acquiring Dalham mill and millhouse he achieved a longstanding ambition to own a mill and hoped eventually to see it restored to working order and to work it himself.

As early as January 1971 it was announced that a grant of £2,450 had been made by the DOE towards the repair of the mill. It was expected that Derek Ogden, the Warwickshire millwright, who had done sterling work in the repair of Chesterton and other mills, would undertake the restoration of Dalham mill, but this was not to be. Mr Ogden left Britain to work abroad and Thompsons of Alford contracted to carry out the necessary work. However nothing much happened. Mr Farrow cleaned out the mill and did some minor work to the interior but the millwrights were busy elsewhere and meanwhile costs were escalating.

On top of this the county council reorganisation was taking place so that there was a lack of continuity at planning level. Mr Farrow originally had an agreement with the old West Suffolk County Council whereby they would be responsible for the main structural rebuilding while he would use skills, learnt from his father and grandfather, to put to order the internal workings of the mill.

With substantial funds now available a large quantity of the necessary timber, including new cant posts, was purchased and delivered to the mill in 1976. Old Mr Thompson had died but his foreman had taken over the business and in July of that year he and his men arrived at the mill to start work; or at least that is what Frank Farrow thought. However, once again his hopes were dashed when, after taking down the sails and dismantling the brakewheel, the millwrights found that the condition of the curb was worse than they had thought. A new curb was needed but this had not been allowed for in the contract and anyway Thompsons were too far committed with other jobs to make one for two years. How the condition of the curb was overlooked at the time of inspection can only be surmised but the new Suffolk County Council invited tenders from other millwrights and in May 1978 a Solihull firm, Gormley and Goodman, commenced what promises to be a long restoration scheme.

At Reydon Quay, near Southwold, the little brick drainage pump has stood derelict for many years. For some time Miss Mary Oakeley, headmistress of nearby St Felix School, had been interested in the mill and on enquiring who owned it found that the school did! In 1970 she contacted the SPS for advice and later that year more than 100 schools in the east of England were asked to submit projects in a European Conservation Year scheme sponsored by the Royal Institution of Chartered Surveyors.

The restoration scheme, put forward by the girls, won a £125 prize as winner of the competition. The schools' League of Social Service donated £70 and a fund was established.[10] A local builder contracted to repair the brickwork of the tower which was breached and badly eroded and this has been done.

Lound towermill was converted into a house in 1961 but in the process lost its machinery and its character. The beautifully elegant boat-shaped cap was replaced by one of extremely crude design.

Tricker's mill at Woodbridge nearly suffered an equally unhappy fate when, in 1974, a scheme for building sheltered homes for the elderly on the surrounding ground threatened the derelict mill's future. Fortunately the outcome was somewhat happier here for, although the mill will never carry sails again, it has retained most of its interesting, late iron machinery and without the crowning ignominy of a 'mock' cap, such as that fitted at Lound, retains a little of its former dignity as well.

Standing at the centre of the development, the ground and first floors of Tricker's mill serve as a common room, TV lounge, and visitors' overnight accommodation with the fine cast-iron bridge trees and tentering gear carefully restored *in situ* as a reminder of the building's former use. A late nineteenth century sifter and a cleaner, situated under the first floor had to be removed. They were carefully dismantled and it is hoped eventually to use them in a working mill.

We have seen how, in various ways, mills have been preserved and restored and how occasionally their use has changed giving them a new lease of life in a different and sometimes, unfamiliar guise.

The future of those examples in the care of the DOE and the County Council is now as certain as it can be. They are less likely to perish from their old enemies, storm and lightning than in their working days.

Apart from the few restored mills there lie in the county well over a hundred lesser remains ranging from derelict towers, containing machinery, to such fragments as foundations, portions of postmill tramways and pieces of millstone.

One of my favourite 'wrecks' which I have watched grow ever more decrepit over the years, is that of the postmill at Eye. Brake and tail-wheels have rotted from the iron windshaft since first I photographed them in 1961 but the fine dated post still stands and, I feel, deserves a place in a local museum.

The next fifty years will see most of the picturesque ruins disappear while a growing awareness of our heritage coupled with greater leisure will hopefully ensure the continuing survival of at least a handful of the preserved examples we can see today.

With reserves of fossil fuels diminishing we might even see a revival of some of the earlier methods of producing power by harnessing the forces of nature. Who knows, a new generation of wind machines may spring up one day, perhaps producing electricity, but with precisely calculated modern design and technology they could never be as quaint and diverse as their corn grinding and water pumping predecessors.

Hopefully a few people will take up repairing Suffolk mills with the same enthusiasm and dedication that is often applied to old houses, steam locomotives and traction engines. Not so long ago mill restoration meant house conversion to most people. Many more mills were then standing, few relevant books were available and knowledge of the subject was very restricted. It is therefore not surprising that so much misguided work was carried out in the names of restoration and preservation.

Today there is no excuse. People generally are better educated and more aware of their surroundings, a number of good books are readily available and several millwrighting firms practise the old crafts. Government departments and local authorities, as well as several societies, will give grant aid to the *sincere* restorer.

The appeal of mill restoration all but defies description. The nearest definition I can give is that of a lady who spent many years beautifully restoring an old house and said of it: 'I regard it as my work of art'.

Appendix A

The following is an estimate by Thos. Bear, millwright, for the building of the tower windmill subsequently erected in Lavenham on the site of an earlier postmill at NGR 915499. It is reproduced by kind permission of Mr A. E. Baker who owns the original.

An Estimate & Agreement made this 9th Day of Sept. 1830 between Mr Thos. Bare Millwright of Bulmer in the County of Essex on the one Part & Mr Robert Lee of Lavenham in the County of Suffolk Miller on the other part, in as much as the said Thos. Bare doeth agree to Build a *Wind Mill* under the following particulars and for the Sum of *Four Hundred & Thirty Pounds*.

4 New Patent Sails 9 Yards & half in length and average 8 ft wide—2 Fir Midlings each 53 ft long 4 fir Clamps for Do. each 22 ft long Iron Bolts & Grufells for Do. Cast Iron Wind Shaft about 30 cwt Iron Chain nick brasses & Bolts for Do. Tail brass Keep & bolts for Do. Iron Rod to go through Do. Shaft Cranks bolts Stay Irons for Head & Shaft—Cast Iron Box Brasses Back Nut Roler poppets Spindle & Wheel to Cloth & uncloth chain & spout for the Chain to work in—The Cap new Elm Curb to lay on Brick Work 15 ft 6 in Diam. 8 by 9—2 Fir Sheer trees each 20 ft long 12 by 12 one Oak Weather Beam 1 Fir head Stock & Fir tail Beam 7 Fir bearers each 4 ft long Fir Crown Beam—Brass Block & Sleepers—Cast Iron Segment to go round the Curb one Inch over inside Wt 14 Cwt with bolts—Iron Bar for inside of Do. Cast Iron rolers & frames to work in the Segment & bolts for Do.—Elm Curb for Roof 17 ft 6 in Diam. 4 by $4\frac{1}{2}$ 2 Oak Weather spars each 13 ft long 4 by 5 at center—New Oak Bale—700 ft Weather Board for Roof Oak Cill 10 ft long 6 by 9 Cast Iron Nut to work in Segment with spindle Brasses Chairs etc. 3 Cast Iron Wheels 3 Nuts & Chairs Brasses Bolts & Cranks—long upwright Spindle with Chairs Brasses Bolts etc.—2 Wheels for top of Do. Flyer Spindle with Chairs & Brasses & Bolts to Do. 6 Flyer Stands & Flyers. Wood for the Stage at Tail of the Mill Top gudgin hoops Chair & Brasses for upright Shaft and Bolts do Do. 2 Gudgin hoops Chairs Brasses Bolts etc. for the Middle of the Shaft one Gudgin hoop & Brass for bottom of Do. Break Wheel 8 ft 6 in high with 79 Cogs Arm New Break & Staff with Irons & Bolts Cast Iron Wallow Nuts 30 Wood Cogs. Iron Fly Wheel with 70 Cogs 2 Cast Iron Stone Nuts Iron spar wheel 5 ft 10 in high with 92 Cogs 2 Stone Spindles—2 Bridge Boxes 2 Step & 4 Neck Brasses 2 Sets of Ballance Irons 2 pair of Brass Collars. One New 4 ft 6 Runner Stone 1 Pair 4 ft 2 Stones New pair vatts with hopper Bearers & Shoe repairing old vatts of Do.—2 Sets of Regulatars with lighter Irons etc. 2 New Damsels Posts poppets & Bridge trees for the stones & upright shaft Flour Mill Nut & Iron Shaft with poppets brass Chairs Brasses & flour Mill & jumpers Rogers with frame and Brasses etc. Old Flour Mill to repair and fix new jumper with spindle Brasses & frame Wood facing to Wallow Nut & drive Sack Tackle. Roll & Rigour with Gudgins hoops poppets brass Chairs Brasses etc. for Do. Tackling for taking Stone Nutts out of work—2 New Corn Schreens all Workmanship Raising the Roof Gearing the Wheels & fixing all the before Mentioned Works in a Workmanship Like Manner and like Wise to find all Proper Irons & Brass for the afor said Work account of Workmenship pulling down the Old Post Mill and fixing one pair of Stones in the Tower Mill to have the Oak Midling for the use of the New Mill & Wind Shaft & Post to use old Bolts & Irons in the new Mill. Also to Receive 2 Sails of Old Mill one Break (sic) wheel and one Running Stone for my own use and to have all the Old Brass all the old Iron.

Mr Lee to find and fix all the Bond Timber all the Girder Joists & floors, Meal Troughs, Spouts, Straps, Ropes, Cords, Hoppers, & Bins, Casing Painting etc. etc.

Thomas Bear agree to do as above and have the Mill in goeing & Grinding Order at the Expireation of Twelve weeks after the Brickwork is Compleated or forfeit the Sum of Thirty Pounds out of the above Mentioned Sum.

Mr Lee agree to lett Thomas Bear have on account of the above mentioned sum the Money according to the Valuation of what may be deliverd or is ready for delivery the Remainder to be payd when the Mill is compleated. Mr Lee allso Aggree to Board and Lodge Thomas Bear dureing the time he is aboute the Mill at Lavenham and to do all the Carting of the above. Thos. Bear to take down the Old Mill at his own expence.

As above we have aggreed and Sett our Hands this Eighteenth Day of September 1830.
witness
Abraham Ray   Robt. Lée
James Andrews   Thos. Bear

It should be noted that the new mill was a large one having sails of $9\frac{1}{2}$ bays on 53 ft (16.16 m) *middlings* or stocks and a curb diameter of 15 ft 6 ins (4.73 m).

The spelling of some of the items is rather quaint; even Bear's name varies! Although not laid out in the detail of William Bear's contract for constructing Buxhall Mill (see Rex Wailes: *The English Windmil*, Appendix C) it is interesting to compare the two. Both were large towermills erected on the site of, and re-using parts of, earlier mills. The contract price for Lavenham was £430 whereas Buxhall, thirty years later, cost £353 odd for materials and £152 for labour, a total of about £506. Buxhall was slightly the larger mill so it is obvious that costs were stable during the middle years of the nineteenth century.

It appears that the above prices were for millwright's work and materials only and that the cost of building the tower was reckoned separately and indeed the tower erected by a builder to the millwright's requirements.

It is interesting to note that the cost of modernising a postmill could approach the figures quoted above. Henley mill, built in 1810, was jacked up and the roundhouse heightened, fitted with new patent sails and set up to drive three pairs of stones in 1837 at a cost of £400. The cost of modernising Framsden mill, the year before, but driving only two pairs of stones, was probably not much less.

Lavenham towermill stood across the road from an earlier towermill demolished *c* 1900. The later mill, which was similar but taller than its neighbour, was dismantled in 1921 after standing derelict for some years and now all that remains is an ivy-clad stump.

Both mills were in the Baker family for many years.

Appendix B

A summary of the expenses for the building of Great Bradley towermill in 1839 was lodged with the West Suffolk Records Office at Bury St Edmunds (ref. E3/10/105.7). This mill was built by R. Hunt of Soham, Cambs. again on the site of an earlier mill as one is recorded here as far back as 1783. Unlike the building accounts for Lavenham and Buxhall mills (see appendix A) this one includes for brickwork but unfortunately for us does not enumerate the separate millwrighting items.:

	£	s	d
Bricks 12000 white bricks @ 36s	21	12	0
23000 red bricks @ 35s	40	5	0
Lime 570 bushell @ 5d	11	17	6
Carting bricks, matls, lime etc.	15	0	0
Brickwork 12 rod 51 ft brickwork @ 38s	23	4	0
153 yds Plastg. and Lime wash incl. hair, etc.	2	11	0
292 Cement wash outside @ ½d		12	2
Taking down and cleaning 10000 old bricks @ 3s 6d	1	15	0
Digging out foundations		10	0
Stone To 24 feet York slab for curb bolts	1	4	0
4 window cills 16 feet @ 2s 6d	2	0	0
2 York slab @ 1s 2d		6	0
28 feet for Landing	1	10	8
A piece of stone over the door		5	0
Painting Mr. Chapple for three times painting— 439 yds 6 feet and 8 dozen 10 ft sashes } @ 7 d	13	8	1
Glazing 45 ft 3 in Crown Glass and Putty @ 1s 4d	3	0	4
Millwright's work Mr R. Hunt's Bill of Extras	14	3	5
	£153	4	2

Contract Paid £435

The name: Anthony Jackson, Esq., Barkway is appended.

It appears that the purchaser was slightly overcharged although if he checked the bill he would soon have realised that two times 1s 2d does not equal 6s!

We don't know who the owner was. None of the trade directories before 1844 lists a miller here but in 1844 the miller was Hanslip Nice and he must have been a young man then, as he was still there thirty years later.

The mill was of medium size and unusual for its age, being winded by means of a handchain and pulley. The miller in 1900 was Josiah Nice but it appears that the mill soon after this went out of use. It lingered on in a thicket of bushes until demolished in 1953. At some time the brickwork must have shown a weakness as four tie rods had been inserted in the upper portion of the tower passing completely through the structure with cast iron plates on the outside of the walls.

Appendix C

The following is a 'Schedule of Goods, Chattles, Furniture, fixtures and Stock in Trade of Thomas King of Wetherden, Miller. Taken 28 Feb. 1775.' The original documents including deeds dating from 1734 are from the Redstone Collection lodged with the Suffolk Records Office (ref. W13— T4/23/1). It reads:

In the Mill

A pair of French stones 4 ft 6 inches high, one ditto 4 foot high, one peake stone 4 foot high, a Boulting Mill with 6 boulting cloths and all spur gares ropes and pullies. Twenty french Bills and five peake ditto. One Iron crow, three hammers, one axe, two shaves, handsaw, four chizzells and gough, three iron spindles and rings eight sacks and four sail cloths.

It is interesting to note that the mill bills used for French (Burr) stones and Peak stones were kept separate and one wonders what their difference might have been. Perhaps the new bills were retained for the French stones until worn to such a degree that they were seconded for use on the less demanding Derbyshire Grit stones used to grind animal feed.

The mill is not mentioned in a deed of 1734 and is first shown on a map in the second edition of John Kirby's *Suffolk Traveller*, published in 1764. The mill was accorded the name Warren Mill and its latterday appearance may be seen from the illustration.

Gazetteer of Suffolk Windmills

TYPE: PR = Post with roundhouse; POT = Post, open trestle; P = Post;
PB = Post, buck only; S = Smock; T = Tower; C = Composite; Tr = Trestle;
IP = Iron Pump; HP = Hollow Post.
M 1783 (e.g.) The earliest map on which the site can be positively identified.

Parish or Town	Mill name or location	Type	Nat. Grid Reference	Date Built	Remarks
Corn Mills					
Aldeburgh		POT	*c* 465565		On map of 1588
,,		POT	*c* 464564		On maps of 1588, 1594
,,		POT	*c* 465572		On maps of 1588 & later
,,	Station Road	PR	460570	1724–25	Demol. 1924
,,	Fort Green	T	465560	M 1824	Conv. to a house 1902
Alderton	Mill Cottages		345424	M 1736	
,,		S	346416	1796?	Demol. 1956
Aldringham		PR	443608	1803	Moved to Thorpeness
All Sts S. Elmham		T	344828	M 1824	Demol. by 1920
Alpheton		PR	878494	M 1824	Demol. 1879
Ashbocking	On the Green	PR	187547	M 1826	Demol. *c* 1895
Assington		POT	933372	1868	Standing 1902
Bacton		PR	044664	1798–9	Blown down *c* 1900
Badingham		P	*c* 308680	M 1824	
,,	Colston Hall	P	*c* 320672		Moved to 320677
,,	Low Street	POT	311688	M 1783	Demol. *c* 1913
,,	New Mill	PR	320677	*c* 1870	Burnt 1922
Badwell Ash		POT	986687	M 1783	Demol. *c* 1930
Bardwell		P	948730	M1783	
,,		T	941737	Dtd. 1823	Sails removed *c* 1925
Barham			*c* 123514	Pre 1815	Belonged to Workhouse
Barking	Mill Lane	S	092541	*c* 1792	Demol. 1918
,,	On the Tye	PR	065521	M 1783	Demol. 1910
Barnby			474898	M 1837	Gone by 1883
Barnham		P	*c* 876786	M 1736	Moved to Stanton
,,		T	868791	1821	Built for Duke of Grafton
Barningham		POT	973769	M 1783	Was clockwise
,,		POT	973768	M 1783	Was anti-clockwise
Barrow	Old Mill	POT	767641	M *c* 1730	Demol. *c* 1883
,,		P	*c* 764638	1801–2	
,,	New Mill	S	765637	M 1824	Demol. 1926

Parish or Town	Mill name or location	Type	Nat. Grid Reference	Date Built	Remarks
Barton Mills			729735	M 1824	
Beccles	Bullock's Mill	P	421896	M 1736	
,,	Hadingham's	T	421898	M 1824	Demol. 1923
,,	Sayer's Mill		423910	M 1826	
,,	Ingate Mill	PR	432897	M 1783	Was standing 1882
,,	Castle Mill	T	425896	M 1838	Replaced by Steam Mill
Bedfield		POT	222664	M 1824	To next site
,,		POT	221663	M 1842	Demol. *c* 1903
Bedingfield		PR	176683	1828	Dismantled 1921
Belstead			133411	M 1838	Burnt 1895
Benhall	On the green	PR	382610	M 1736	Demol. 1921–2
,,			*c* 380601	M 1736	
Bentley			112368	M 1826	Gone by 1881
Beyton		P	934629	M 1837	Brought from Wickhambrook
Bildeston		P	996491	1798	Gone by 1887
Blaxhall	Dyke's Mill	PR	369572	M 1783	Burnt 1883
Blundeston		T	516975	*c* 1820	Last worked 1923
Blythburgh	Prior's Mill	P	*c* 453742	M 1736	Rebuilt in 1782
,,		S	453749	M 1824	12-sided. Demol. 1937
Botesdale			*c* 049761	M 1764	No details
,,		PR	047756	M 1817	Dismantled before 1885
,,	Lodge Mill	PR	054757	1777?	Demol. *c* 1916
,,		S	049755	M 1885	Moved from Palgrave; Demol. *c* 1918
,,	Black Mill	T	058750	*c* 1854	Demol. 1909
,,			052762	M 1783	No details
Boxford	Calais Street	PR	972402	M 1824	Gone by 1885
,,	Cherry Ground	PR	9723397	M 1783	Was standing in 1885
,,	Whitestreet Green	PR	974392	M 1824	Gone by 1885
,,		S	959402	M 1783	Burnt 1901
Boxted	Fenstead End	S	806509	M 1783	
Boyton		PR	378470	M 1824	Burnt *c* 1910
Bradfield St George		P	922587	M 1826	Believed demol. *c* 1860
,,		S	923585	M 1824	Demol. 1943
Bradwell		PR	510042	M 1736	Was standing in 1903
Bramfield		PR	404739	M 1826	Demol. *c* 1904
,,		P	398753		Preceded towermill
,,	Waterloo Mill	T	398753	1815	Dismantled 1944 for scrap metal
Brandeston		PR	246610	*c* 1810	Burnt 1893
Brandon	Mill Hill		788858	M 1736	
,,	New Mill Piece		791862	M1838	On Tithe Map
Brantham	Near Stutton Watermill		129331	M 1826	Went *c* 1880
Bredfield		POT	270536	*c* 1804	

Parish or Town	Mill name or location	Type	Nat. Grid Reference	Date Built	Remarks
Bredfield		PR		Pre 1800	
,,		T	272529	M 1838	Demol. 1919 or 20
Brent Eleigh		P	938476	M 1805	Demol. 1895
,,	Town Hill Mill		940475	M 1826	
Brettenham		P	955537	M 1783	Preceded smockmill
,,		S	955537	1804	Demol. after 1939
Brockley	Mill Hill House		829562	M 1783	
,,	On the green	PR	825547	M 1824	Demol. 1930
Brome		PR	135762	M 1824	Dismantled *c* 1900
Bruisyard			328662	M 1783	
,,		P	329665	M 1837	
Brundish		POT	257702	M 1824	Demol. 1920
,,	Upper Mill	PR	264698	M 1783	Demol. *c* 1914–18
Bungay	Flixton Road	P	337892	M 1826	Demol. 1879
,,		S	337890	M 1826	Blown down 1864
,,	Sayer's Mill	T	336895	M 1826	Burnt 1868
,,			*c* 338894	M 1783	Standing 1826
,,		P	340895	M 1783	Standing 1824
,,	Upland Mill	PR	339887	M 1838	Demol. 1918
,,		T	338890	M 1826	Last worked 1918
,,			*c* 342896	M 1764	No details
Burgh	in same yard	T	230514	M 1826	Small
,,		T	230514	1842	Sails removed *c* 1919
Burgh Castle		T	487040	M 1837	Demol. *c* 1925
Bury St Edmunds	Mill Road	P	849641	M 1783	Standing 1867
,,	Tayfen Meadows		848655	M 1824	Blown down
,,	Kings Road	P	847641	M 1675	Moved to Wickhambrook
,,	Kings Road	S	847642	M 1836	Demol. *c* 1913
,,	Southgate Mill	PR	861628	M 1783	Disused by 1903
,,	Nowton Road	T	861627	1836	The 6-sailer
,,		PR	860630	M 1740	Disused in 1845
,,	West Mill	PR	842632	M 1783	Demol. 1918
,,	Eastgate Mill	PR	*c* 864645	Pre 1597	Standing 1688
Butley		PR	385515	M 1783	Burnt
,,		PR	385515	1842	Working *c* 1883
Buxhall		P	998577	M 1783	Burnt 1814
,,	on same site	S	998577	1815	
,,		T	998577	1860	Sails removed 1930
Campsey Ash			*c* 319550	M 1783	
,,		PR	320560	M 1820	
Capel St Mary	Windmill Hill	PR	083383	M 1826	Demol. 1909
,,		S	088381	1848	Demol. 1886
Charsfield		P	249561	M 1783	
,,			256569	M 1824	
,,		PR	256570	M 1824	Demol. 1917
Chattisham	on same site	S	090425	M 1838	
,,		S	090425	1867?	Demol. after 1947
Chedburgh			790576	M 1824	
Chediston		T	346776	M 1826	Demol. 1925

Parish or Town	Mill name or location	Type	Nat. Grid Reference	Date Built	Remarks
Chelmondiston	Elmer's Mill	PR	200374	M 1783	Demol. 1913
Chevington		PR	784594	M 1783	Out of use before 1900
Clare	Mill Hill	POT	775454	M 1678	
,,			762446	M 1783	Blown down 1875
,,	Chilton Street	T	757472	Post 1846	Working *c* 1883
Claydon		PR	132502	M 1783	Working 1892
Cockfield		PR	901545	M 1783	Demol. after 1902
,,		P	901542	M 1783	Blown down 1860
,,		S	896554	M 1826	Not shown on 1837 OS
,, }	Pepper Mill	T	904539	M 1826	
,, }	on same site	T	904539	1891	Ceased work *c* 1900
Coddenham }	on same site	P	135544	M 1785	
,, }		PR	135544	1810–11	Demol. 1909
Combs	Upper Mill	PR	020538	M 1736	
,,	Branstead Mill	PR	035557	M 1736	Demol. after 1931
Copdock		P	*c* 115411	*c* 1810	
Corton		P		Pre 1793	Was standing 1848
,,		T	542974	*c* 1801?	Ceased work before 1914
Cotton		PR	068672	M 1783	Demol. *c* 1915
Cowlinge		S	714537	M 1824	Demol. 1955
Cransford		S	329651	M 1837	Moved to Peasenhall
Cratfield	Bell Green	PR	308755	*c* 1824	Blown down 1879
,,	North Green	PR	304768	Post 1842	Buck top to Huntingfield
Creeting St Mary			113578	M 1837	No details
,,		P	095558	*c* 1796	Buck still existing
,,	Creeting Bottoms		117582	M 1764	No details
Creeting St Peter		P		*c* 1800	No details
Cretingham		POT	233603	M 1837	
,,		T		pre 1834	Was standing 1860
Crowfield		S	151571	M 1883	Brought from the marshes
Culford		P	*c* 825696	M 1783	
,,	At the watermill	P	821700	M 1836	No details
Dalham		S	719617	pre 1803	Last worked 1926
Darsham		POT	420693	M 1783	Moved to next site
,,		PR	415702	1801	Demol. 1937
Debach		PR	248556	M 1824	Stood on a mound
Debenham		POT	171638	M 1826	Demol. *c* 1890
,,	Page's mill	PR	182638	M 1736	Demol. *c* 1917
,, }	on same site	P	165630	M 1736	
,, }		T	165630	1839	Dismantled 1962
Denham		PR	195740	M 1783	Demol. 1910
Dennington		POT	278669	Pre 1804	Moved to Trimley St Martin
		PR	286670	*c* 1822	Demol. 1925
Depden	On the green	PR	776575	M 1783	Demol. *c* 1910
Drinkstone	Mill Farm	P		Pre 1780	No details

Parish or Town	Mill name or location	Type	Nat. Grid Reference	Date Built	Remarks
Drinkstone		PR	964622	1689	Preserved
,,		S	964621	*c* 1780	Last worked *c* 1900
Dunwich		POT			On map of 1587
,,		POT			On map of 1587
Earl Soham		POT	247644	1849	Brought from Ipswich
,,	Ashfield mill	PR	219634	Pre 1739	Demol. 1947
,,		PR	227628	M 1783	Dismantled 1947
Earl Stonham	Bell's Cross	POT	089598	M 1824	Wrecked 1908
,,	,,	PR	090597	M 1824	Demol. 1905
East Bergholt		PR	084350	Pre 1779	One known as The Black Mill and one,
,,		PR	083349	Pre 1779	The White Mill
Edwardstone	Mill Green	S	952426	M 1783	
Elmsett	Mill Farm	PR	055461	M 1824	
,,		P	054463	M 1838	Moved to Offton
,,	Ladbrook's mill	PR	048465	*c* 1830	Dismantled 1929
Eriswell		S	723801	post 1839	
Exning			625658	M 1783	No details
Eye	Castle Mound	POT	147738	M 1783	Moved to Cranley Green
Eye	Cranley Green	PR	160726	*c* 1845	Dismantled 1917
,,		S	146740	M 1837	To Occold
,,	Hayward's Mill	T	160736	M 1837	Ceased work *c* 1916
,,	Victoria Mill	PR	139742	1779	Collapsed 1955
Eyke		PR	318521	M 1783	Dismantled 1910
Felixstowe	Ferry Road		*c* 318363		Had gone by 1740
Felsham		P	944571	M 1824	Moved to Gedding 1867
Finningham		P	067686	M 1783	Demol 1877
Flowton		S	083469	M 1838	Demol. *c* 1910
Fornham St Genevieve		P	832692	M 1783	Stood on a tumulus
Fornham St Martin		POT	848672	M 1824	Moved before 1882
,,		S	849671	M 1836	Blown down *c* 1926
Fornham St Martin			*c* 859663	M 1783	No details
Framlingham	Lodge Farm	S	265643	*c* 1890	Moved from Hacheston
,,		S	283631	M 1736	
,,	Saxmundham Rd	PR	292635	M 1826	Demol. 1884
,,	Mount Pleasant	PR	279638	M 1824	Demol. *c* 1927
,,	Mount Pleasant	P	278638	M 1736	Moved to Tannington
,,		POT	283630	M 1826	On same site
,,	Victoria Mill	T	283630	1843	Demol. 1935
Framsden	Ashfield Place	S	200614	*c* 1820	On same site
,,		PR	200614	*c* 1882	Demol. 1922
,,		PR	192598	*c* 1760	Preserved
Freckenham		S	662716	Pre 1781	Believed demol. *c* 1910
,,		S	661720	*c* 1823	Demol. 1967
Fressingfield	Algar's Mill	POT	255774	M 1884	Demol. *c* 1895
,,		PR	254772	M 1826	Demol. *c* 1929
,,	Chippenhall Grn	PR	287759	M 1783	Demol. 1936

Parish or Town	Mill name or location	Type	Nat. Grid Reference	Date Built	Remarks
Friston		PR	412601	c 1811	Ceased work 1959
Gazeley		POT	718649	M 1824	Blown down after 1844
,,		T	717649	1844	Ceased work c 1910
Gedding		POT	956576	M 1783	Demol. c 1904
,,		PR	957576	1867	From Felsham; Demol. 1944
Gisleham		PR	512867	Pre 1807	Burnt 1911
Gislingham	Allwood Green	PR	048717	M 1783	Said to be dated 1615
,,	Mill Street		c 070720	M 1826	No details
,,	Mill Street	T	067720	1821	Demol. 1930
Glemsford			833480	M 1799	No details
,,	Weston Mill		833466	M 1826	No details
Gosbeck		P	160555	M 1826	On same site
,,		PR	160555	1865 or 1868	Dismantled 1924
Gt Ashfield	Button Haugh Green	PR	990665	M 1783	Demol. c 1917
Gt Barton		PR	882678	M 1783	Demol c 1920
Gt Bealings		P	236486	c 1810	
Gt Bradley			665534	M 1783	On same site
,,		T	665534	1839	Demol. 1949
Gt Bricett		P	038504	M 1783	On same site
,,		S	038504	1851	Demol. 1954
Gt Cornard			884410	M 1805	
,,			c 884407	M 1805	one was a postmill with roundhouse
,,			885402	M 1805	
Gt Finborough		PR	010563	Pre 1814	Disused by 1884
Gt Thurlow		P	672500		On same site
,,	Collis's Mill	S	672500	1807	Last worked by wind 1920
Gt Waldingfield		S	906438	M 1824	Demol. 1912
Gt Welnetham	Chapelhill Mill	PR	889586	c 1801	Demol. c 1914
,,		PR	880578	M 1783	Demol. c 1949
,,	Clarke's Mill	T	878598	1865	Sails blown off 1916
Gt Wratting			699488	Pre 1780	Had gone by 1840
Gt Yarmouth	High Mill	T	519074	1812	Demol. 1904–5
(Southtown which was	Green Cap Mill	T	517074	c 1815	Burnt 1898
transferred to Norfolk	Water's Mill	PR	516077	M 1783	
in 1891)					
,,	Halfway House	T	523055	M 1764	
,,	Church Road	T	526047	M 1826	
,,	Cliff Mill	T	529035	M 1837	Demol. 1887
Grundisburgh		PR	224505	1807	Demol. c 1934
,,		S	c 221507	c 1885	A working model
Hacheston		P	307594	M 1826	No details
,,		S	312567		To Framlingham
Hadleigh			c 025433	M 1824	No details
,,	Mill Hill	P	016447	M 1783	To Elmsett or Whatfield

Parish or Town	Mill name or location	Type	Nat. Grid Reference	Date Built	Remarks
Hadleigh		S	035428	M 1783	Last worked 1905
Halesworth	Gothic Mill	P	387773	M 1837	
,,	Broadway	P	394790	Pre 1844	Working 1878
,,	Pound Hill	P	384769	M 1783	Demol. pre 1900
,,	Pound Hill	C	383769	M 1783	Demol. *c* 1905
,,	Calver's Mill	PR	385777	1788	Demol. 1942
,,	Mill Hill	S	*c* 385777	*c* 1810	With the postmill
Hargrave		S	770604	M 1783	Gone by 1914
Hartest			838520	M 1836	No details
,,		PR	826520	M 1783	Burnt down *c* 1958
Hasketon			242503	M 1824	No details
,,	Goddard's Mill	T	241501	M 1824	Demol. 1925
Haughley	On the Green	PR	030644	M 1783	Demol. *c* 1896
,,	Mere Mill	PR	029625	M 1824	Burnt *c* 1900
,,		PR	031622	1811	Burnt 1940
Haverhill	Mill Hill		669451	M 1824	No details
,,	Castle Mill	PR	663457	M 1824	Demol. 1901
,,	Mill Road	T	671452	M 1824	
,, ⎱	on same site	P	674460	M 1793	Conv. to a composite
,, ⎰		T	674460	*c* 1855	Demol. 1942
Henley		PR	155515	1810	Burnt 1884
Hepworth		POT	995743	M 1783	A clockwise mill
Higham	Nr Hadleigh		032361	M 1805	No details
Higham	Nr Newmarket	T	*c* 745655	M 1824	Demol. *c* 1885
Hinderclay ⎱	on same site	P	021766	M 1824	No details
,, ⎰		T	021766		Demol. *c* 1935
Hintlesham		PR	095436	1807?	Working in 1880s
Hitcham	Millhill Farm	POT	998545	M 1902–4	Tiny Farm mill; near an old site
,,		PR	986514	M 1783	
,,	Cross Green	T	991531	M 1824	Demol. *c* 1925
Hollesley		PR	342435	M 1783	Blown down 1881
,,			352447	M 1826	Gone by 1880
Holton St Peter		PR	403773	Pre 1750	Preserved
Honington		P	912738	M 1837	
,,		PR	911739	M 1837	A tall, large mill
Hopton			*c* 987798	M 1826	Moved to 998801
,, ⎱	close together	PR	998801	M 1783	
,, ⎰		PR	998801	1834	Demol. *c* 1912
Horham		POT	208724	1750	Demol. 1934
Hoxne		P	192776	M 1736	
,,	Chase's Mill	PR	192777	M 1826	Demol. 1923
,,	Cross Street	POT	186762	M 1824	Buck to Worlingworth
Hundon	Mansfield's Mill	POT	735492	M 1783	Demol. *c* 1928
,,	Brockley Mill	POT	721470	M 1824	Disused in 1905
,,	Savage's Mill	PR	718470	M 1884	Disused in 1905
Hunston	Mill Hill		*c* 980676		Moved to Badwell Ash

Parish or Town	Mill name or location	Type	Nat. Grid Reference	Date Built	Remarks
Huntingfield	Barrell's Mill	POT	335749	M 1824	
,,	Whitehouse Farm	P	*c* 327743		Moved to 321745
,,	Aldridge's Mill	PR	321745	*c* 1879	Demol. 1928
Icklingham			778726	M 1826	No details
Ilketshall St Andrew	Mill Common	P	376877	one	In same yard
,,		P	375877	M 1783	
Ilketshall St Lawrence		T	378840	1812	Part demol. *c* 1914
Ipswich		POT	*c* 173443	M 1674	
,,	Town Marshes		*c* 160442	Pre 1733	near each other; both gone by 1812
,,				*c* 1733	
,,	Bishops Hill	PR	176438	M 1736	Moved to Offton
,,	Foxhall Road	P	191440	M 1812	Gone by 1885
,,	Sidegate Lane		179454	M 1838	Went *c* 1870
,,	Stoke Hill	P	159437	M 1736	To Earl Soham 1849
,,		PR	160437	M 1764	Demol. 1887
,,	Stoke Green	P	165435	M 1812	Went *c* 1849
,,	Belstead Road	P	154431	M 1812	Standing 1866
,,	Halifax	P	163425	M 1812	Close together
,,	,,	PR	163425	M 1838	
,,	Bolton Mill	P	162457	M 1812	Standing 1848
,,	Folly Mill	S	172456	M 1812	To Kettleburgh *c* 1855
,,	Anglesea Road	S	159453	M 1826	Standing 1848
,,	,,	PR	157452	1806	Burnt 1859
,,	Albion Mill	PR	175453	one	Working in 1882
,,	,,		175452	M 1805	Was gone by 1882
,,	North Hill Road	T	173449	M 1783	Went *c* 1886
,,	Bank Road		174451	M 1848	Was gone by 1855
,,	Bellvue Road	PR	176449	M 1764	Standing 1873
,,	Woodbridge Road		*c* 177450	M 1826	No details
,,	,,		*c* 177451	M 1826	No details
,,	Bramford Road	T	149452	Pre 1844	Tower demol. *c* 1959
,,	Lattice Lane	S	189448	Pre 1881	Demol. *c* 1930
,,	Lower Orwell St	P			On painting of 1753
Ixworth			*c* 941703	M 1783	
,,			924711	M 1824	Gone by 1882
,,			936708	M 1826	One was built in 1825
,,			941692	M 1826	
Kedington		PR	701464	M 1838	Was disused in 1902
,,		T	702469	M 1783	Demol. 1945
Kelsale	Dorley's Corner	PR	385660	M 1764	Dismantled 1923–24
,,	Carlton		*c* 386642	M 1783	No details
Kelsale	Carlton	PR	381647	1815?	Moved from Aldeburgh?
,,	,,	T	382647	1856	Last worked *c* 1910
Kersey	Williams Green	T	990425	M 1824	Demol. 1907
Kessingland			*c* 517865	M 1783	No details
Kettleburgh		S	267598	*c* 1855	Ceased work 1872 or 73
Knodishall			*c* 416604	M 1783	No details

Parish or Town	Mill name or location	Type	Nat. Grid Reference	Date Built	Remarks
Knodishall	Coldfair Green	PR	434610	M 1836	Demol. 1908
Lakenheath			719829	M 1783	
,,	Claypits	T	710817	M 1824	Worked in 1914–18 war
,,			719822	M 1880	No details
,,			721820	M 1880	No details
Lavenham		P	915499	M 1783	Prior to towermill
,,		T	915499	1830–31	Demol. 1921
,,		P	917486	M 1783	Gone by 1883
,,		T	916499	M 1824	Gone by 1883
Lawshall	Golden Lane	P	847551	M 1824	No details
Laxfield	Mill Field	P?	c 295741		No details
,,	Winks Lane	P?	300723	M 1783	No details
,,	Banyard's Green	P	304730	M 1826	No details
		PR	293722	M 1736	Demol. c 1941
,,	Gorham's Mill	S	295728	1842	Demol. after 1939
Layham		P?	025393	M 1826	Gone by 1884
,,		T	038402	M 1824	Demol. c 1900
Leavenheath		PR	955372	M 1805	Demol. 1925
Leiston	Monastic Mill	POT	c 447625	Pre 1608	Demol. c 1870
,,	Valley Road	S	446628	M 1837	Demol. 1917
Letheringham		P	280580	M 1826	Moved to Charsfield
Levington	On the heath	PR	245403	M 1783	
Lidgate			718576	M 1824	Gone by 1884
Lit. Glemham		POT	357584	M 1824	Buck to Theberton
Lit. Stonham		T	114600	M 1884	Dismantled 1908
Lit. Thurlow		P	675516	M 1736	
,,		S	677507	1865	Last worked c 1909
Lit. Waldingfield		P	918447	Pre 1693	Last shown on Greenwood
Lit. Wratting			699471		Converted to steam c 1869
Long Melford		POT	857465	Pre 1758	Went c 1887
Lound ⎱		PR	499006	M 1736	
,, ⎰	on same site	T	499006	1837	Last worked 1939
Lowestoft	Gunton Mill	P	c 548944	M 1650	Stood in 1751
,,	Church Road	T	544942	M 1751	Demol. c 1899
,,	Cleveland's Mill	T	543924	M 1803	
,,	Foxe's Mill	T	543922	M 1826	
,,			c 551946	M 1736	
,,	Brickworks		532939	M 1882	No details
Market Weston		POT	980775	1807	Demol. c 1911
Marlesford		PR	330581	M 1824	Last worked c 1896
Martlesham		T	249464	1820	Demol. c 1890
Mellis	On the green	POT	086738	M 1783	Demol. c 1898
Melton		PR	275506	c 1800	
,,			c 286512	Pre 1801	
Mendham		P		c 1802	Advertised for sale in 1805
Mendlesham	Mill Terrace	POT	096634	M 1824	Gone by 1884

Parish or Town	Mill name or location	Type	Nat. Grid Reference	Date Built	Remarks
Mendlesham		S	*c* 102660	Pre 1781	
,,	Ling's Mill	PR	090634	M 1783	Demol. *c* 1918
,,	Kersey's Mill	PR	092638		From Otley Demol. 1926 or 27
,,	Kent's Mill	PR	102656	M 1824	Partly demol. 1910
,,	On the green	P	*c* 098630	M 1824	
Metfield		PR	295806	M 1824	
,,		PR	300798	M 1783	
,,	Office Farm	T	302793	1839	Partly demol. 1916
Mettingham		POT	363905	1826	Gone by 1836
Middleton		PR	427676	M 1783	Dismantled before 1914
Monewden		PR	241585	M 1837	Demol. *c* 1928
Monks Eleigh		P	974474	M 1783	
,,		P	963481	M 1837	
,,		P	965480	M 1799	
Monk Soham	Broadway	C	207658	M 1837	Moved to next site
,,		C	207663	Pre 1883	Demol. 1937
,,			*c* 199670	M 1824	No details
Mutford		PR	486881	M 1826	Demol. 1923
Nacton		P	221406	M 1826	
Nedging	With the watermill		993477	M 1805	Gone by 1884
,,	Naughton Mill	PR	017496	M 1824	Burnt 1909
Needham Market		S	085556	M 1764	Demol. *c* 1880
Newmarket		P	*c* 640630	Pre 1669	
,,	Langley's Mill	S	637638	Pre 1780	Demol. 1934
Newton	On the green	S	919402	M 1826	Disused by 1885
Norton		P	956656	pre 1806	
,,	The Street	P	957671	M 1837	Demol. *c* 1906
Oakley	By the watermill	P	170769	M 1736	To Bedingfield 1828
Occold ⎱			156705	M 1826	
,, ⎰	on same site	S	156705		From Eye. Disman. 1921
Offton ⎱	close together on boundary with	P	073495	M 1881/3 ⎱	One from Ipswich
,, ⎰	Willisham	P	*c* 073494	⎰	one from Elmsett
Old Newton		P	055623	M 1783	
,,	Ward Green	S	048643	M 1837	Demol. *c* 1896
Onehouse	Union Mill	PR	032591	1801 or 2	Was standing 1882
Orford		POT	418506	M 1736	Demol. 1913
,,	Black Mill	PR	422503	M 1820	Burnt *c* 1886
Otley		P	195552	M 1837	To Mendlesham
,,	Chestnuts' Mill	S	213562	M 1824	Demol. *c* 1908
,,	Davey's Mill	PR	203551	M 1837	Dismantled *c* 1912
Oulton Broad	Lady Mill	T	522930	M 1736	Demol. 1932
,,	Knight's Mill	T?	521930	M 1841	Gone by 1903
Ousden		S	742598	M 1826	Collapsed *c* 1880
,,		POT	725599	M 1826	Blown down before 1914
Pakefield		PR	536904	M 1783	Demol. 1888
Pakenham	Nr the watermill		*c* 936696	M 1783	No details

Parish or Town	Mill name or location	Type	Nat. Grid Reference	Date Built	Remarks
Pakenham			*c* 917676	M 1824	
,,		T	931694	1831	Preserved
Palgrave	Mill Lane	S	116781	M 1837	Moved to Botesdale
,,		S	122776	Rebuilt 1803	Demol. *c* 1937
Parham	Mill Green	PR	313612	Dtd. 1821	Demol. *c* 1944
Peasenhall		PR	351695	1803/4	Dismantled *c* 1957
,,	close together	S	351695	*c* 1882	From Cransford; engine powered
Pettaugh		POT	167595	M 1783	
,,	rebuilt on same site	PR	167595	Rebuilt 1865	Dismantled 1957
Pettistree		T	305552	M 1820	Demol. *c* 1898
Polstead	Bower House Tye	POT	990411	M 1883	From Stoke by Nayland?
,,			988375	M 1805	Worked with watermill
Preston		S	*c* 943509	M 1826	
,,		P	940507	M 1824	Gone by 1902
,,		P	941507	M 1824	Gone by 1883
,,		T	942508	Dtd 1846	Demol. 1928
Rattlesden	Mill Hill	P	976590	Pre 1805	Probably on same site
,,		T	976590		
,,		S	968583	M 1783	Demol. *c* 1900
,,		T	968582	*c* 1850	
Raydon	Near the watermill			Pre 1793	Was 'timber built'
Redgrave			*c* 038788	M 1826	No details
,,		POT	039786	M 1783	Demol. *c* 1903
,,		T	039782	M 1824	Burnt 1923
Redlingfield	Mill Farm	POT	182713	M1824	Blown down 1881
Reydon		P		*c* 1800	Burnt by 1803
Rickinghall Inferior		PR	039759	M 1783	Down *c* 1885
Rishangles	Wright's Mill	C	164674	M 1783	Burnt 1903
Rougham	Mill Heath	PR	916644	M 1698	Was disused 1882
Rumburgh		POT	348812	Pre 1814	Blown down *c* 1870
Rushmere St Andrew		S	201457	1814	Burnt *c* 1939
St Cross S. Elmham	(Sancroft)		297836	M 1826	Gone by 1883
St James S. Elmham		PB	320814		Went 1972
,,	close together	PR	320814	1864	From Starston, Norfolk
St Michael S. Elmham		PR	338841	1799	Demol. 1955
Sapiston		P	*c* 924744	M 1736	
Saxmundham		PR	383631	M 1824	Dismantled 1907
Saxtead		PB	253644		From Orford
,,	in same yard	PR	253644	Pre 1796	Preserved
Shadingfield		PR	434848	M 1764	Demol. *c* 1905
,,		S	411844	*c* 1840	Demol. 1938–9
Shimpling			*c* 863524	M 1783	
,,	Mill Hill	PR	859519	M 1783	Moved *c* 1875
,,	The Street	S	872530	Dtd 1792	Dismantled 1935
Shotley		POT			Shown on print of 1730

Parish or Town	Mill name or location	Type	Nat. Grid Reference	Date Built	Remarks
Shotley		T	224361	M 1826	Last worked *c* 1880
Shottisham		P	320445	M 1838	
Sibton		PR	366693	M 1736	Dismantled 1922–23
Snape	Turning Mill		403584	*c* 1828	A woodworking mill
,,	Markin's Mill	POT	400582	M 1824	Demol. 1922
,,		PR	394583	Dtd 1668	Dismantled 1933
Somerleyton		P	481969	M 1783	Went *c* 1880
Somersham		POT	085485	Pre 1811	Was standing in 1881
Sotterley	Hulver Street	PR	466868	M 1736	Gone by 1914
Southwold	White or Town Mill	POT	504760	Pre 1723	
,,	Black or Great Mill	PR	504762	1798	Demol. 1894
,,	Baggott's Mill	PR	509762	1841	Burnt 1876
Stansfield }	on same site		785528	M 1783	
,,		T	785528	1840	Cap removed 1922
Stanstead		PR	844490	M 1799	Blown down *c* 1915
Stanton	Bury Lane	P	963731	M 1824	Standing 1882
,,	Upthorpe	PR	971733	Dtd 1807	Last worked *c* 1945
,,		S	962736	M 1764	Demol. *c* 1939
,,	Stanton Chair	PR	963742	1824	Dismantled after 1915
Stoke Ash		PR	114694	M 1764	Burnt 1883
Stoke by Clare			*c* 737438	M 1783	
,,		T	724435	M 1824	Demol. *c* 1890
,,		PR	744438	M 1824	Demol. 1892
Stoke by Nayland	Next to watermill		012357		Standing 1884
,,			*c* 007362	M 1783	No details
,,	Withermarsh Green	PR	006369	M 1824	
Stonham Aspall	Mill Green	PR	137603	M 1826	Dismantled 1909
Stowmarket }	at south of town			M 1675 }	no details
,,				M 1675 }	
,,		PR ?	046593	M 1824	Gone by 1884
,,		PR	044593	M 1824 }	Both disused by 1903
,,		PR	045594	M 1824 }	
,,	Fison's Mill	S	042585	M 1824	Burnt 1884
Stowupland		P	*c* 074600		
,,	Mill Street		*c* 066591		No details
,,		PR	063598	Pre 1802	Dismantled 1866
,,	On the green	T	067598	M 1824	Demol. 1919
Stradbroke	Battlesea Green	POT	223754	M 1813	Burnt 1898
,,	Barley Green	PR	240740	*c* 1704	Demol. 1940 or 41
,,	Skinner's Mill	PR	228743	Dtd 1688	Demol. 1941
Stradishall		PR	740531	M 1783	Demol. 1884
Stratford St Andrew		PR	356602	M 1824	Dismantled 1905
Sudbury		POT	*c* 882419	pre 1614	Also on plan of 1714
,,		P	880414	M 1805	To Assington 1868
,,		T	873417	M 1824	
,,		T	871417	M 1824	
,,	Highfield Mill	S	866429	1855	Conv. to a house 1927
Sutton		PR	317458	M 1838	Blown down *c* 1916
Swefling	Girling's Mill	PR	348639	Dtd 1775	Dismantled 1935
,,	Middle Mill	PR	350640	M 1783	Dismantled after 1899

Parish or Town	Mill name or location	Type	Nat. Grid Reference	Date Built	Remarks
Swefling	High Mill	PR	351640	M 1783	Dismantled 1911
Swilland		PR	190538	M 1824	Dismantled c 1953
Syleham		PR	214777	c 1823	Moved from Wingfield
Tannington		P	252681	c 1855	From Framlingham; Blown down 1879
Theberton	together	PB	440657		From Lit. Glemham
,,		T	440657	Pre 1756	Dismantled c 1923
Thelnetham		P	011790?	M 1783	To Diss Nfk. 1818
,,		T	011790	1819	Last worked c 1930
Thetford	Now in Norfolk		860821	M 1836	
Thorndon		PR	139698	1797	Dismantled 1924
Thornham Magna		PR	110711	M 1675	Burnt 1959
Thurston		PR	916661	1750	Demol. c 1953
Trimley St Martin	Mill Lane	PR	272379	M 1783	Demol. after 1918
,,	,,	T	273380	M 1881	Disused by 1902
,,	Kirton Road	PR	276389	M 1807	Dismantled 1918
Troston		S	896733	M 1824	Demol. c 1885
Tuddenham St Martin		PR	190484	Pre 1782	Demol. c 1901
Tuddenham St Mary		S	729720	M 1783	Disused in 1901
Tunstall		PR	372548	c 1808	Demol. 1928–29
Ubbeston		PR	319718	M 1837	Dismantled 1924
Ufford		P	c 303525	c 1840	Moved to Worlingworth
,,		S	294530	c 1888	Moved to Hacheston
,,		T	298532	M 1820	
Uggeshall		PR	447800	M 1736	Demol. 1923
Walberswick		PR	496746	M 1838	Blown down c 1923
Waldringfield		PR	280444	c 1806	Dismantled c 1916
Walpole		PR	366748	M 1736	Blown down 1919
Walsham-le-Willows	Crowland Mill	P	005703	M 1783	Was standing 1884
,,		PB	005718	c 1890	From Wortham
,,	together	PR	005718	M 1824	Dismantled 1917
Walton	Ferry Lane	P	287344	M 1806	Went c 1858
,,	Wadgate Mill	PR	290345	M 1804	Went c 1890
Walton		S	290359	M 1806	Dismantled c 1903
Wangford		PR	470796	M 1736	Demol. c 1917
,,		S	468790	M 1883	Burnt 1928
Wattisfield		PR	013745	M 1783	Demol. 1914
Wenhaston			415769	Pre 1793	On top of watermill
,,	Blackheath	PR	425747	M 1783	Demol. c 1896
,,	Kitty Mill	PR	420758	M 1837	Buck dismantled c 1967
Westerfield	probably the same mill	S	170475	Pre 1795	Moved to nearby site below
,,		S	170474	c 1819	Went by 1880
Westhall	Mill Common	PR	409816	M 1824	Dismantled 1957
,,	together	PB	409816	1928	From Huntingfield
Westleton	Rouse's Mill	POT	445683	M 1736	Was burnt
,,		PR	444692	M 1842–3	Demol. 1963
,,	Ralph's Mill	S	444685	M 1783	Tower demol. 1969

Parish or Town	Mill name or location	Type	Nat. Grid Reference	Date Built	Remarks
Weston		PR	410862	M 1837	Burnt 1896
Wetherden		PR	007630	M 1824	Went after 1914
,,	Warren Mill	PR	997629	M 1764	Demol. *c* 1907
Wetheringsett	Old Mill Green	PR	131650	M 1783	Demol. 1919
,, }	Broad Green	PR	145649	M 1826	Blown down 1881
,, }	same site	PR	145649	1882	Dismantled 1957
,,	Brockford Green		*c* 124653	M 1824	No details
Weybread	Shotford Heath	P	*c* 246815	M 1736	
,,	,,		*c* 224795	M 1826	No details
,,		P	232808	M 1826	To Framsden *c* 1882
,,		P	256799	M 1826	Moved to next site?
,,	Nr Dranes' Farm	PR	257801	M 1884	Demol. *c* 1926
Whatfield		POT	026465	Post 1844	Disused by 1884
Whepstead	Mickley Green	PR	841579	M 1783	Burnt 1894
Whitton cum Thurlston		T	143475	M 1838	Was working 1892
Wickhambrook	Bullock's mill	PR	743552	M 1836	Demol. 1909
,,	Great Mill	PR	751540	Dtd 1740	Finally cleared away 1966
,,	Fuller's mill	PR	756555	*c* 1850	From Bury St Edmunds
,,	Baxter's Green	P	*c* 762583	M 1824	Moved to Beyton *c* 1830
Wickham Market	Charsfield Road		298562	M 1824	Gone by 1881
,,	,,		299562	M 1824	Gone by 1881
,,		P	303561	M 1881	Gone by 1902
,,	Mill Lane	S	305556	*c* 1778	Dismantled *c* 1885
,,		T	305566	M 1783	Demol. 1868
Wickham Skeith	Wickham Street	POT	093697	M 1826	Moved to next site
,,	Wickham Green	POT	*c* 092693		Demol. 1881
,,		T	094692	*c* 1870	Demol. 1925
Wingfield	Earsham Street	P	234782	M 1837	Went *c* 1910
,,	,,	POT	234782		Moved to Syleham
Wissett		T	375786	M 1837	Demol. *c* 1920
Withersfield		POT	658472	M 1783	Demol. *c* 1910
Witnesham	Wood Farm	POT	183519	M 1826	Demol. *c* 1888
,,		POT	183504	*c* 1815	Burnt *c* 1908
Woodbridge	Mill Hills	P	270496	Pre 1819 }	3 shown on
,,	,,	P	270495	Pre 1819 }	Hodskinson's map of
,,	,,	P	270494	Pre 1819 }	1783. One still standing
,,	,,	P	271494	Pre 1819 }	1866
,,	Victoria Road	T	274494	*c* 1825	Stump stood *c* 1905
,,	Drybridge Hill	PR	263491	M 1820	
,,	Theatre Street	PR	268491		Roundhouse stood *c* 1930
,,	Tricker's mill	T	268491	1818–19	Last worked *c* 1920
,,	Buttrum's mill	T	264493	1816–17	Last worked 1928
Woolpit		P	*c* 995622	M *c* 1568	No details
,,	Pyke's mill	PR	976622	Dtd 1644	Demol. 1924
,,	Elmer's mill	PR	968627	M 1675	Collapsed 1963
Worlingworth	Honeypots Farm	PB	223706		From Hoxne

Parish or Town	Mill name or location	Type	Nat. Grid Reference	Date Built	Remarks
Worlingworth	Old Mill	PR	213688	M 1783	Dismantled *c* 1914
,,	New Mill	PR	212688	1848	Demol. 1952
Wortham	Magpie Green	PR	070784	M 1881	To Walsham-le-Willows
,,	Wortham Ling	PR	091796	M 1783	Demol. 1917
,,		S	081768	M 1826	Demol. 1948
Wrentham	Mill Lane	POT	*c* 503826	M 1736	Moved to next site
,,	Fletcher's mill	POT	496822	M 1783	Collapsed 1931
,,	Carter's Mill	PR	499819	M 1824	Demol. 1955
,,		T	499823	M 1837	Tower demol. 1964
Wyverstone		P	035673	M 1837	
,,	Black Mill		031677	M 1884	No details
Yaxley		T	121737	M 1824	Burnt *c* 1885
Yoxford		PR	395681	M 1764	
,,		PR	396682	*c* 1813	Dismantled after 1910
,,			*c* 395687	M 1783	No details

Drainage Mills and Pumps

River Lark

Parish or Town	Mill name or location	Type	Nat. Grid Reference	Date Built	Remarks
Fornham All Saints			834685	M 1882	No details
Freckenham	Lee Brook		665749	M 1881–6	Gone by 1901
Mildenhall	White Top Mills	S	619811	M 1783	Standing 1927
,,			620812	M 1820	Standing 1885
,,	Cross Bank		623806	M 1824	Was standing 1905
,,			623801	M 1783	Gone by 1885
,,			*c* 624799	M 1783	No details
,,			*c* 629790	M 1783	Replaced with engine by 1885
,,			*c* 631790	M 1783	
,,	Middle Mill	S	631786	M 1820	Dismantled after 1905
,,	Mill Drain Mill		637774	M 1820	Gone by 1885
,,	West Row		662753	M 1836	Gone by 1885

Lit. Ouse River

Parish or Town	Mill name or location	Type	Nat. Grid Reference	Date Built	Remarks
Lakenheath	Turf Fen Mill	S	692838	M 1824	Standing 1881
,,		S	673851	M 1854	Gone by 1881
,,	Crosswater's Mill		677855	M 1783	Gone by 1854
,,			*c* 673857	M 1824	No details
,,	Great Fen Mill	S	678855	M 1881	Demol. *c* 1949

River Waveney

Parish or Town	Mill name or location	Type	Nat. Grid Reference	Date Built	Remarks
Barnby	Hober Mill		487918	M 1826	No details
Barsham		T	400910	M 1838	Base remained in 1927
Beccles			437926	M 1838	Replaced by engine *c* 1880
Belton	Black Mill	T	468035	M 1837	Dismantled 1942
,,			475032	M 1883	No details
,,			476026	M 1883	No details
,,			477035	M 1883	No details
Blundeston		T	499952	M 1826	Disused by 1900
Bradwell			512060	M 1883	No details

Parish or Town	Mill name or location	Type	Nat. Grid Reference	Date Built	Remarks
Burgh Castle		T	489064	M 1826	
,,			475037	M 1883	No details
Carlton Colville	Share Mill		494928	M 1837	Replaced with engine by 1883
Fritton		T	450998	M 1837	Working 1937
,,	Fritton Warren	Tr	453008	1910?	Demol. *c* 1948
,,	Caldecott Mill	T	465021	M 1783	Working 1937
Gt Yarmouth	Cobholm Island	T	511075	M 1837	Standing 1886
Herringfleet		S	466976	M 1826	
,,	St Olave's	S	457998	M 1884	Demol. 1898
,,		Tr	457998	1910–12	On site of smock
Lowestoft			543930	M 1863	Gone by 1882
North Cove		T	465911	M 1882–3	
,,	Black Mill		470912	M 1882–3	
,,			476919	M 1783	No details
,,	Castle Mill	T	479922	M 1837	Replaced with engine by 1883
Oulton	Skepper's Mill	Tr	502937	M 1835–6	
,,	Arnold's Mill	T	501945	M 1783	Ceased work by 1903
Oulton Broad		T	516928		No details
Somerleyton		T	480959	M 1837	Turbine Pump
Worlingham		T	453914	M 1835–6	Replaced with engine by 1883
Coastal Marshes					
Aldeburgh		HP	461562	M 1851	Standing 1882
,,	Thorpe Road	S	468582	*c* 1800	Demol. *c* 1900
,,			465583	M 1903	No details
,,	Corporation Marshes	S	451555	M 1881–2	Gone by 1902
Dunwich			476707	M 1882–3	No details
,,	Corporation Marshes		486732	M 1897	Iron pump in 1957
Gedgrave	Chillesford Lodge	T	399502	M 1820	
Minsmere		S	475659	M 1897	
(Leiston parish)					
,,		IP	475659	*c* 1920	On site of smock
,,	Seawall Mill	S	477662	M 1826	Collapsed 1976
,,	Eastbridge	S	468662	M 1903	Collapsed 1977
Orford		P			Buck went to Saxtead
Reydon	Blackshore Mill	T	491759	*c* 1890	A plunger pump
Sizewell		IP	474645	M 1897	
,,		IP	475621	M 1897	No details
,,	'Old draining pump'		474641	M 1884	Gone by 1903
Walberswick	Westood Marshes	T	487737	M 1897	
,,			478762	M 1903	
,,	Tinker's Marshes		490756	M 1882	Gone by 1925
Miscellaneous					
Bury St Edmunds	Waterworks	IP	849642	1899 or 1900	Demol. *c* 1940
Creeting St Peter	W. Creeting Green		078582	M 1903	With reservoir
Gt Cornard		HP?	882399		A model?
,,		S	893394	M 1881–5	

Parish or Town	Mill name or location	Type	Nat. Grid Reference	Date Built	Remarks
Gt Cornard			884407	M 1902	No details
Hundon	Clare Waterworks		741497	M 1902	No details
Leiston		T	444628	M 1881	Gone by 1903
Sotterley	Brickworks		450842	M 1883	Gone by 1903
Southwold	Salt Works	HP	507757		Standing 1938
,,	On the Common	IP	502763	*c* 1886	
Thorpeness		HP	468598	1922–23	From Aldringham
,,	'Kursaal'	HP	473597	*c* 1911	Taken from a shipwreck
West Stow	Sewage Works	IP	803712	*c* 1898	A Titt engine

List of Suffolk Windmill Remains

TYPE: PR = Post with roundhouse; POT = Post, open trestle; P = Post;
PB = Post, buck only; S = Smock; T = Tower; Tr = Trestle;
IP = Iron pump; HP = Hollow Post.

Parish or Town	Mill name or location	Type	National Grid Reference	Description of Remains
Corn Mills				
Aldeburgh	Fort Green	T	465560	Tower incorporated in a house
Alderton		S	346416	Foundations only
All Sts S. Elmham		T	344828	Stump is a chicken shed
Badingham	New Mill	PR	320677	Part of roundhouse roofed
Badwell Ash		POT	986687	Shed made from rebuilt buck
Bardwell		T	941737	Derelict with cap frame but no sails
Barnham		T	868791	Converted into a house; no cap
Bedingfield		PR	176683	Roundhouse used as a store
Blundeston		T	516975	Tower an empty shell
Brome		PR	135762	Roundhouse contains the up shaft
Bungay		T	338890	Converted into a house; no cap
Burgh		T	230514	Tower only; no machinery
Bury St Edmunds	Kings Road	S	847642	Foundations only
Buxhall		T	998577	Tower only; no machinery
Chattisham		S	090425	Foundations only
Chelmondiston		PR	200374	Concrete tramway visible
Chevington		PR	784594	Roundhouse used as a store
Clare	Chilton Street	T	757472	Tower an empty shell
Cockfield		T	904539	Tower only; no machinery
Combs	Upper Mill	PR	020538	Roundhouse used as a store
Corton		T	542974	Tower only: no machinery
Creeting St Mary		P	095558	Buck now stands at 091553
Crowfield		S	151571	Derelict; no cap but some machinery
Dalham		S	719617	Preserved; to be restored
Darsham		PR	415702	Roundhouse used as a store
Debenham		T	165630	The two storied stump a store
Dennington		PR	286670	Lower part of roundhouse walls
Drinkstone		PR	964622	Preserved; used to drive a saw
Drinkstone		S	964621	Derelict; no sails or machinery
Earl Soham		PR	227628	Roundhouse converted to a house
Elmsett		PR	048465	Roundhouse incorp. in modern mill
Eriswell		S	723801	The base used as a store
Eye	Cranley Green	PR	160726	Shortened roundhouse used as store
Eye	Victoria Mill	PR	139742	Collapsed remains
Eyke		PR	318521	Broken down roundhouse walls
Framlingham		S	283631	The base converted into a house

Parish or Town	Mill name or location	Type	National Grid Reference	Description of Remains
Framsden		PR	192598	Preserved with 2 sails
Freckenham		S	662716	The base used as a store
Freckenham		S	661720	Foundations remain
Fressingfield		PR	254772	Roundhouse used as a store
Friston		PR	412601	Preserved without sails
Gazeley		T	717649	Converted into a house
Gosbeck		PR	160555	Roundhouse used as a store
Gt Thurlow		S	672500	Preserved
Gt Welnetham		PR	880578	Fragments of roundhouse
Gt Welnetham	Clarke's Mill	T	878598	Derelict without cap or sails
Grundisburgh		PR	224505	Roundhouse converted into a house
Hadleigh		S	035428	Part of base incorp. in Mill House
Hartest		PR	826520	Fragments of roundhouse
Hasketon	Goddard's Mill	T	241501	Part of foundations
Haverhill	Mill Road	T	671452	Stump used as a store
Holton St Peter		PR	403773	Preserved; has no machinery
Honington		PR	911739	Roundhouse converted into a house
Horham		POT	208724	Foundations visible
Huntingfield	Aldridge's Mill	PR	321745	Fragments of roundhouse
Ilketshall St Lawrence		T	378840	Tower an empty shell
Kelsale		PR	385660	Roundhouse used as a store
Kelsale	Carlton	PR	381647	Foundations visible
Kelsale	Carlton	T	382647	Tower only; no machinery
Lakenheath	Claypits	T	710817	The stump an empty shell
Lavenham		T	915499	The stump an empty shell
Laxfield	Gorham's Mill	S	295728	The base used as a store
Lit. Stonham		T	114600	The stump an empty shell
Lit. Thurlow		S	677507	The base converted to a house
Lound		T	499006	Converted into a house
Mendlesham	Kent's mill	PR	102656	The roundhouse used as a store
Mendlesham	Ling's mill	PR	090634	Foundations only
Metfield		PR	300798	Lower part of roundhouse walls
Metfield	Office Farm	T	302793	The stump an empty shell
Middleton		PR	427676	Foundations only
Nedging	On the Tye	PR	017496	Foundations only
Occold		S	156705	The base used as a store
Otley	Davey's mill	PR	203551	Derelict roundhouse
Pakenham		T	931694	Preserved complete
Peasenhall ⎫	close together	PR	351695	The roundhouse used as a store
Peasenhall ⎭		S	351695	The power mill in the tower disused
Preston		T	942508	Foundations only
Rattlesden		S	968583	Part of base incorporated in power mill
Rattlesden		T	968582	Derelict without cap or sails
Rougham	Mill Heath	PR	916644	Derelict roundhouse with trestle
St James S. Elmham		PR	320814	Roundhouse used as a store
St Michael S. Elmham		PR	338841	Lower part of roundhouse walls
Saxmundham		PR	383631	Roundhouse part of garage premises
Saxtead		PR	253644	Preserved complete
Shimpling	The Street	S	872530	The base used as a store

Parish or Town	Mill name or location	Type	National Grid Reference	Description of Remains
Sibton		PR	366693	Roundhouse used as a store
Snape		PR	394583	Roundhouse converted into a house
Stansfield		T	785528	Derelict without cap or sails
Stanstead		PR	844490	Part of roundhouse walls
Stanton	Upthorpe	PR	971733	Derelict with 2 sails
Stanton	Stanton Chair	PR	964742	Roundhouse converted into a house
Stoke by Nayland	Withermarsh Gn	PR	006369	Roundhouse used as a store
Stonham Aspal	Mill Green	PR	137603	Roundhouse used as a store
Stradbroke	Barley Green	PR	240740	Roundhouse used as a store
Stratford St Andrew		PR	356602	Roundhouse used as a store
Sudbury	Highfield Mill	S	866429	The base converted into a house
Swefling	Girling's Mill	PR	348639	Roundhouse used as a store
Swefling	Middle Mill	PR	350640	Roundhouse converted into a house
Swefling	High Mill	PR	351640	Fragments of roundhouse
Swilland		PR	190538	Roundhouse used as pottery studio
Syleham		PR	214777	Derelict with 2 sails
Theberton		T	440657	The stump an empty shell
Thelnetham		T	011790	Derelict with 2 sails
Thorndon		PR	139698	Roundhouse used as a store
Thornham Magna		PR	110711	Foundations visible
Trimley St Martin		PR	276389	Roundhouse converted into a house
Tuddenham St Mary		S	729720	Foundations dumped nearby
Tunstall		PR	372548	Tramway only
Ubbeston		PR	319718	Lower part of roundhouse walls
Walsham le Willows		PR	005718	Roundhouse in use as power mill
Walton		S	290359	Derelict; no cap or machinery
Wenhaston	Blackheath	PR	425747	Base of roundhouse walls
Wenhaston	Kitty Mill	PR	420758	Roundhouse converted into a house
Westhall		PR	409816	Roundhouse used as store
Westleton	Rouse's mill	POT	445683	Four piers; one overturned
Westleton	Ralph's mill	S	444685	The lower brick base only
Westleton		PR	444692	Foundations remain
Wetheringsett	Broad Green	PR	145649	Roundhouse used as a store
Wichambrook	Bullock's mill	PR	743552	Piers and remains of roundhouse walls
Wickham Market	Mill Lane	S	305556	The stump an empty shell
Woodbridge	Tricker's mill	T	268491	Tower, containing some machinery, preserved
Woodbridge	Buttrum's mill	T	264493	Preserved with 4 sails
Worlingworth	Old Mill	PR	213688	Roundhouse used as a store
Worlingworth	New Mill	PR	212688	Foundations only
Yoxford		PR	396682	Roundhouse converted into a house

Drainage Mills & Pumps

River Lark

Mildenhall	Middle Mill	S	631786	The base converted into a house

Lit. Ouse River

Lakenheath	Great Fen Mill	S	678855	Base of walls remain

Parish or Town	Mill name or location	Type	National Grid Reference	Description of Remains
River Waveney				
Belton	Black Mill	T	468035	Derelict tower with cap
Fritton	Caldecott Mill	T	465021	Derelict tower with cap
Fritton		T	450998	Derelict tower
Herringfleet		S	466976	Preserved complete
Herringfleet	St Olave's	Tr.	457998	Preserved with 2 sails
Oulton	Arnold's mill	T	501945	15 ft (4.5 m) High Stump
,,	Skepper's mill	Tr.	502937	5 brick piers stand
Somerleyton		T	480959	Derelict stump
Coastal Marshes				
Aldeburgh	Thorpe Road	S	468582	Foundations only
Gedgrave	Chillesford Lodge	T	399502	Base of walls
Minsmere		IP	475659	Derelict
Minsmere	Seawall Mill	S	477662	Base walls
Minsmere	Eastbridge	S	468662	Brick foundations
Reydon	Blackshore Mill	T	491759	Tower preserved
Walberswick	Westwood Marshes	T	487737	Burnt out shell with some machinery
Miscellaneous				
Southwold	On the Common	IP	502763	The water tower stands
Thorpeness		HP	468598	Preserved complete

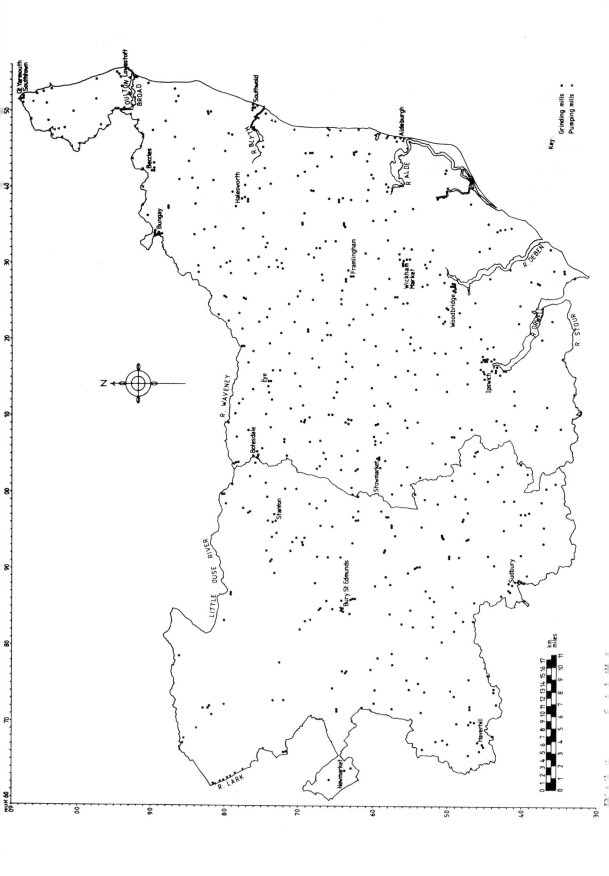

Key: Grinding mills •
     Pumping mills ▲

Gt Yarmouth
Southtown
Lowestoft
OULTON
BROAD
Beccles
R. BLYTH
Southwold
Halesworth
R. ALDE
Aldeburgh
Bungay
Framlingham
Wickham
Market
R. DEBEN
Woodbridge
R. ORWELL
R. STOUR
Eye
R. WAVENEY
Botesdale
Stowmarket
Ipswich
Stanton
Bury St. Edmunds
LITTLE OUSE RIVER
Sudbury
Haverhill
Newmarket
R. LARK

N

km.
miles
0 1 2 3 4 5 6 7 8 9 10 11 12 13 14 15 16 17
0 1 2 3 4 5 6 7 8 9 10 11

Glossary

In most cases terms have been described in the text. More comprehensive glossaries may be found in such standard works as *The English Windmill* by Rex Wailes and *Windmills and Millwrighting* by Stanley Freese. The following selected glossary serves to identify some of the unexplained terms found in this book.

Angle of weather The twist in a sail to give driving power.

Bran The hard cellulose coating of the wheat grain.

Canister The iron box at the head of the windshaft through which the sail-stocks were passed.

Collar A wooden steady bearing encircling the post under the buck of a postmill.

Cullin stone A millstone of lava from Germany which used to be shipped from Cologne; one may be seen as a doorstep at Drinkstone postmill.

Cross or *spider*. The iron casting mounted on the front end of the *striking rod*, which passes through the windshaft to effect shutter control.

Damsel The iron forging which shakes the feed shoe of underdriven stones.

Edge runner A millstone running on its edge about a horizontal axis.

Floats The paddles of the scoop-wheel of a drainage mill.

Fork-iron Rod controlling the two sail-rods of a double-shuttered sail.

Hollow postmill A postmill in which the drive is taken down through the centre of the post by a vertical shaft.

Hurst frame Framework to support the millstones above floor level.

Middlings Coarse flour sometimes with adhering bran particles.

Peak stone A relatively soft millstone, quarried in the Peak District, and used for milling animal feed.

Pit wheel The driven gearwheel mounted on the scoop wheel shaft of a drainage mill.

Power mill A mill driven with machinery powered by steam, oil, gas or electricity.

Prick-post The vertical post supporting the centre of the *weather beam* of a postmill.

Quant The spindle carrying the *stone nut* driving an overdrift millstone.

Shoe The inclined trough feeding grain from the hopper to the stones.

Sprattle beam A fixed beam carrying the thrust bearing of a vertical shaft.

Stone nut The final driven gear pinion in the drive to the stones.

Swing pot A self-aligning neck bearing to the windshaft.

Triangles Triangular cranks imparting the motion of the *cross* to the sail-rods, to control the shutters of Patent sails.

Weather beam or *Breast beam*, the main beam supporting the windshaft.

Whip Backbone of a sail which is attached to the stock.

Wood-wears Wooden blocks around post in buck bottom floor which act as a steady bearing.

Bibliography

Arnott, W. G., *Orwell Estuary* (Ipswich 1966)

Bacon, Nathaniel, *Annals of Ipswich* (Reprinted Ipswich 1884)

Bennett, Richard and Elton, John, *History of Corn Milling* Vol. 2 Watermills and Windmills (1899; reprinted Wakefield 1973)

Buckland, J. Stephen, Jones, David H. and Major J. K., editors, *Millnotes* (Published privately 1970–1974)

Cobbett, William, *Rural Rides* (1830; reprinted London 1908)

Darby, H. C., *The Draining of the Fens* (Cambridge 1956)

Defoe, Daniel, *Tour Through The Eastern Counties* (1724; reprinted Ipswich 1949)

Freese, Stanley, *Windmills and Millwrighting* (Cambridge 1957, reprinted Newton Abbot 1971)

Gillingwater, E., *An Historical Account of the Ancient Town of Lowestoft* (1790; reprinted Lowestoft 1897)

Higgins, Pearce, *A Short History of Boxford* (unknown)

Hills, Richard L., *Machines, Mills and Uncountable Costly Necessities* (Norwich 1967)

Hollingworth, A. G. M., *History of Stowmarket* (Ipswich 1844)

Hoskins, W. G., *The Making of The English Landscape* (9th edn., London 1970)

Kelly, W. & Co., *Post Office Directory of Suffolk* (1846, 1854, 1869, 1879, 1883, 1888, 1900, 1904, 1912 etc.) Also directories for Ipswich.

Kirby, John, *The Suffolk Traveller* (2nd edn., 1764)

Pigot, J. & Co., *Directories of Suffolk* (1830 and 1839)

Redstone, Lilian J., *Ipswich Through The Ages* (Ipswich, 1948)

Redstone, V. B., *Annals of Wickham Market* (Woodbridge 1896)

Reynolds, John, *Windmills and Watermills* (London 1970)

Salmon, John, *Journal of the Archaeological Association*, V. XXIX, 1966

Scarfe, Norman, *The Suffolk Landscape* (London 1972)

Storck, John and Teague, Walter Dorwin, *Flour for Man's Bread* (Minneapolis 1952)

Templeton, W., *The Operative Mechanics Workshop Companion* (1858)

Wailes, Rex, *The English Windmill* (London 1954)
    Windmills In England (London 1948)
    Transactions of the Newcomen Society
    1941–42 'Suffolk Windmills Pt. 1—Post Mills'
    1942–43 'Suffolk Windmills Pt. 2—Tower Mills'
    1955–56 and 1956–57 'Norfolk Windmills Pt. 2—Drainage and Pumping Mills Including
      Those of Suffolk'
    1964–65 'Suffolk Watermills'

White, Lynn Jnr., *Medieval Technology and Social Change* (Oxford 1962)

White, William Ltd., *History, Gazetteer and Directory of Suffolk* (1844, 1855, 1874, 1885, 1892; the
    1844 edn. reprinted Newton Abbot 1970)

Woolford, A., *Suffolk Institute of Archaeology Proceedings* (1929)

Young, Arthur, *General View of the Agriculture of The County of Suffolk* (1794; 1813 edition
    reprinted Newton Abbot 1969)

References

Chapter 1

1 *The Chronicle of Jocelyn de Brakelond*, reprinted in Thomas Carlyle's *Past and Present* 1843
2 *Medieval Technology and Social Change* by Lynn White Jnr. Oxford 1962 p.87
3 In Normady Ibid
4 *The Making of the English Landscape* by W. G. Hoskins Hodder and Stoughton 9th Edn. 1970
5 Per Mr J. M. Ridgard
6 1080–86. A list of Domesday mills is given in *Watermills and Windmills* by R. Bennett and J. Elton. Reprinted Wakefield 1973
7 *Rural Rides* by William Cobbett 1830
8 As recounted by the late Mr H. G. Cobbold
9 'Suffolk Watermills' by Rex Wailes. Transaction of the Newcomen Society 1964–65
10 The number varies slightly on different copies of the map
11 This number includes 24 drainage mills
12 'Suffolk Windmills Pt. 1—Post Mills' by Rex Wailes. *Transactions of the Newcomen Society* 1941–2
13 'Suffolk Windmills Pt 2—Tower Mills' by Rex Wailes. *Transactions of the Newcomen Society* 1942–3

Chapter 2

1 Several mills are known to have had six quarter bars and three cross trees but none was in Suffolk
2 Thirteenth century Account Rolls for Framlingham—information from Mr J. M. Ridgard
3 From Mr E. E. Burroughes of Botesdale, whose father told him this rhyme
4 *Evening Star* 13 January 1972
5 Saxtead mill previously had two governors
6 A jumper was mentioned as early as 1814 in an advertisement for the sale of a postmill at Walton, near Felixstowe (*Suffolk Chronicle* 2 April 1814)
7 Information from Mr W. Clover, owner
8 The Diary of Thomas King of Thelnetham
9 *Claydon Rural Deanery Magazine* December 1884
10 *Windmills and Millwrighting* p. 154 by Stanley Freese (Newton Abbot 1971)
11 *Rural Rides* by William Cobbett (London 1908)
12 'Suffolk Windmills Pt. 1—Postmills' by Rex Wailes *Transactions of the Newcomen Society* 1941–42
13 *Orwell Estuary* p. 15 by W. G. Arnott (Ipswich 1966)
14 *The Suffolk Landscape* p. 96 by Norman Scarfe (London 1972)
15 Deeds to the mill property in the hands of the owner, Mr Piers Hartley
16 Correspondence with Mr J. E. Wightman

Chapter 3

1 'A Note on Early Tower Windmills' by John Salmon. *Journal of the Archaeological Association* XXIX 1966
2 'The World's Highest Windmill' by Martin H. Press. *Edgar Allen News* June 1951 and correspondence in subsequent issues
3 *Ipswich Journal* 8 October 1836
4 Haverhill Mill: New Light on its Origin by H. E. S. Simmons *Millnotes* No. 1, p. 9—11 October 1970
5 *Ipswich Journal* 12 May 1804
6 'Suffolk Windmills Pt. 2—Towermills' by Rex Wailes *Transactions of the Newcomen Society* 1942–3
7 *Milling* 24 February 1894
8 *History, Gazetteer and Directory of Suffolk* by William White Ltd. 1891–2
9 *Diary of Thos. King of Thelnetham*
10 *Ipswich Journal* 10 April 1830
11 *Ipswich Journal* 12 November 1803
12 *Rural Gleanings* by Orlando Whistlecraft 1851. Reprinted in *East Anglian Miscellany* 1954

Chapter 4

1 *History of Corn Milling Vol. II* by Richard Bennett and John Elton (Wakefield 1973)
2 *Annals of Ipswich* by Nathaniel Bacon (Ipswich 1884)
3 *Suffolk Chronicle* 1 July 1815
4 *Ipswich Journal* 28 March 1801 and 10 January 1801
5 *The English Windmill* by Rex Wailes (London 1954)
6 *Ipswich Journal* 31 October 1812
7 *A Short History of Boxford* by Pearce Higgins n.d.
8 *Ipswich Journal* 7 November 1795
9 *Ipswich Journal* 14 November 1795
10 *Ipswich Journal* 28 December 1799
11 *Ipswich Journal* 13 March 1824
12 *History of Stowmarket* by Hollingworth n.d.
13 *East Anglian Daily Times* 21 January 1944
14 *Ipswich Journal* 17 and 24 January 1784
15 Personal Correspondence
16 SRO Redstone Catalogue 50/20/1.2
17 Lummis Collection. Ipswich Libraries (now lodged at SRO)
18 *Ipswich Journal* 10 October 1789
19 *Ipswich Journal* 22 November 1806
20 *Ipswich Journal* 3 December 1803
21 *Ipswich Journal* 11 June 1825
22 *Ipswich Journal* 13 October 1821
23 *Ipswich Journal* 28 May 1825
24 *East Anglian Daily Times* 14 January 1890
25 *The History of Ipswich* by G. R. Clarke 1830 p. 257–60
26 *East Anglian Daily Times* 22 January 1890
27 *Ipswich Journal* 2 June 1787

28 *Ipswich Journal* 17 March 1866
29 Much of this information gleaned from *Annals of Wickham Market* by V. B. Redstone (Woodbridge 1896)
30 See account in *Windmills and Millwrighting* by S. Freese (Newton Abbot 1971)
31 *Ipswich Journal* 18 August 1810
32 Diary of Thos. King of Thelnetham
33 *Suffolk Institute of Archaeology Proceedings* 1929. A. Woolford
34 *The Operative Mechanics Workshop Companion* by W. Templeton (1858)

Chapter 5

1 Cambridge 1956
2 *Map of the County of Cambridge, and Isle of Ely* surveyed by R. G. Baker in the years 1816, 17, 18, 19 and 20
3 'Norfolk Windmills Pt. II: Drainage and Pumping Mills Including Those of Suffolk' by Rex Wailes. *Transactions of the Newcomen Society*, XXX 1955–56 and 1956–57
4 The term 'Burnt Fen' referred to the practice of *Paring and burning* to increase fertility
5 1813, reprinted Newton Abbot 1969
6 *Machines, Mills & Uncountable Costly Necessities* by Richard L. Hills, Norwich 1967, p. 76
7 *General View of the Agriculture of the County of Suffolk* by A. Young, p. 183–4.
8 *An Historical Account of the Ancient Town of Lowestoft* by E. Gillingwater (1790, reprinted 1897) p. 177
9 Ibid. p. 15
10 *Tour Through The Eastern Counties* by Daniel Defoe (1724, reprinted Ipswich 1949) p. 89
11 *Fitch Collection of Illustrations* Vol IX Ipswich Libraries
12 I am indebted to Mr Phillip Unwin, The Mill, Poltesco, Cornwall for much of the historical information on this mill as well as several others
13 *History, Gazetteer and Directory of Suffolk by Wm. White 1844* (Newton Abbot 1970) p. 397
14 *Directory of Suffolk* by Kelly 1846.
15 An article in the *Halesworth Times* 25 January 1968
16 This photograph is reproduced in Rex Waile's paper, 'Suffolk Watermills', *Transactions of the Newcomen Society* XXXVII 1964–65

Chapter 6

1 *Guide to Herringfleet Smock Mill* published by Suffolk County Council (latest edition 1975)
2 *The Story of Pakenham Mill* by John Bryant, edited by Granville Wood (1964)
3 *Evening Star* (Ipswich) 19 January 1961
4 *East Anglian Daily Times* 11 January 1956
5 *Evening Star* (Ipswich) 21 November 1962
6 *Evening Star* (Ipswich) 21 July 1965
7 *The Protection of Structures Against Lightning* C.P. 326:1965
8 *East Anglian Daily Times* 14 August 1970
9 *East Anglian Daily Times* 28 October 1970
10 *Halesworth Times & Southwold Mercury* 10 December 1970

Index

Some of the earliest recorded windmills in Europe were built in Suffolk, and since the Middle Ages Suffolk has beeen a county where windmills predominated. In the 1830s there were over 430 windmills in the county, but the advent of steam and oil engines and roller mills meant that there was a rapid decline in the numbers later in the nineteenth century. Brian Flint's survey lists all the surviving mills and mill remains, and explains the technicalities of how the different kinds of mill worked, emphasising the particular local types and developments. He also describes the life of the millers and the work of the millwrights, and ends with an account of the restoration work done in recent years on a handful of the best surviving mills. There are over seventy illustrations, many previously unpublished, working drawings of three mills, and a distribution map.

75 illustrations

£7.95

BOYDELL PRESS
an imprint of Boydell & Brewer Ltd
PO Box 9, Woodbridge, Suffolk IP12 3DF *and*
27 South Main Street, Wolfeboro NH 03894-2069

ISBN 0-85115-251-1

9 780851 152516